MW01199859

Arthur L. Finkle

Trenton's Jews

Beginning, Adaptation and Achieving the American Dream

Hadassa Word Press

Impressum / Imprint

Bibliografische Information der Deutschen Nationalbibliothek: Die Deutsche Nationalbibliothek verzeichnet diese Publikation in der Deutschen Nationalbibliografie; detaillierte bibliografische Daten sind im Internet über http://dnb.d-nb.de abrufbar.

Alle in diesem Buch genannten Marken und Produktnamen unterliegen warenzeichen-, marken- oder patentrechtlichem Schutz bzw. sind Warenzeichen oder eingetragene Warenzeichen der jeweiligen Inhaber. Die Wiedergabe von Marken, Produktnamen, Gebrauchsnamen, Handelsnamen, Warenbezeichnungen u.s.w. in diesem Werk berechtigt auch ohne besondere Kennzeichnung nicht zu der Annahme, dass solche Namen im Sinne der Warenzeichen- und Markenschutzgesetzgebung als frei zu betrachten wären und daher von jedermann benutzt werden dürften.

Bibliographic information published by the Deutsche Nationalbibliothek: The Deutsche Nationalbibliothek lists this publication in the Deutsche Nationalbibliografie; detailed bibliographic data are available in the Internet at http://dnb.d-nb.de.

Any brand names and product names mentioned in this book are subject to trademark, brand or patent protection and are trademarks or registered trademarks of their respective holders. The use of brand names, product names, common names, trade names, product descriptions etc. even without a particular marking in this work is in no way to be construed to mean that such names may be regarded as unrestricted in respect of trademark and brand protection legislation and could thus be used by anyone.

Coverbild / Cover image: www.ingimage.com

Verlag / Publisher:
Hadassa Word Press
ist ein Imprint der / is a trademark of
OmniScriptum GmbH & Co. KG
Bahnhofstraße 28, 66111 Saarbrücken, Deutschland / Germany
Email: info@hadassa-wp.com

Herstellung: siehe letzte Seite /
Printed at: see last page
ISBN: 978-3-639-79444-1

Copyright © 2016 OmniScriptum GmbH & Co. KG
Alle Rechte vorbehalten. / All rights reserved. Saarbrücken 2016

DEDICATION

I dedicate this book to my grandparents who immigrated in the 1880's and who instilled a deep love of Jewish heritage. I also am indebted to my wife's great grandparents who emigrated from Germany in the 1850's.

To Trenton's immigrant daughters and sons who shared their families' struggles and successes in adapting to America. These reminisces led to the revitalization of the Trenton Historical Society.

To my beloved family: my wife, Linda, my sons, Andrew and Daniel, my grandchildren, Julia and Joshua, and my daughter-in-law Heather. Thanks for being patient with me during this busy time and for allowing me to follow my passion.

ACKNOWLEDGEMENT

I would like to express my gratitude to the many people who helped me complete this work, particularly to Peter Reintitz and the Library of Congress for helping with the images, and to Hadassa Word Press and my editor, Elena Djima, who with care, expertise and patience brought this work to fruition.

TABLE OF CONTENTS

PROLOGUE

Born and schooled in Trenton history and Trenton Jewish traditions, my intent is to trace Trenton Jewry from 1850 to approximately 1957 in a small industrial city with easy transportation connections between Philadelphia and New York. As the industrial revolution swept the United States, Trenton became prominent in manufacturing steel coil, iron and potteries. Trenton's German Jews, not wanting to interfere with the manufacturers and their workers, became successful merchants.

The Great Immigration (1881-1914) of Russian Jews carried on the tradition of merchandizing, beginning with simple peddling to becoming merchant princes in this small city. These merchants serviced the numerous manufacturing workers (and some of their employers) by providing newly created household items necessary in the Consumer Era.

Figure 1. Trenton's Industrial City in 1900

1

This account will explore Trenton, as a small industrial city; the arrival of the German Jews in the 1850's; and the Great Jewish immigration of 1881-1914 in which thousands of mainly Russian, Polish, Hungarian and Romanian Jews sought refuge in Trenton. Then, the story delves into the immigrant period: its people, its institutions, its work and its eventual economic success.

Later, the story line explores the Second Generation of this community, along with the older, smaller German Jewish community and the amalgamating influences of the Young Men's Hebrew Association (YMHA) and other secular organizations 'Americanizing' the Jewish community.

BEGINNINGS

The small city of Trenton was a backwater town in a backwater state. During the Revolutionary War, there were 2,500 people residing in Trenton. As the industrial revolution utilized the natural advantages of Trenton's industrial and transportation resources, so did the population increase. In 1830, Trenton's population was 3,000. Its core industries were iron, ceramics and rubber.

As the industrial revolution progressed, so did Trenton's manufacturing productivity. In 1847, The Cooper-Hewitt Iron Works became first in the United States to roll wrought iron beams to fireproof buildings. Utilizing wrought iron became the rage to decorate the entrances of houses and business during this period and later. Trenton's largest employer was Roebling Steel and Cable employing more than 3,500 workers.

Figure 2. Golden Gate Bridge: Roebling Masterpiece

Schooled as a civil engineer in Royal Polytechnic School of Berlin, John A. Roebling began to produce strong rope initially made of hemp. He then developed a process to make much extremely powerful commercial and residential steel cable. Using these materials, he constructed several bridges and aqueducts. He engineered the railroad to traverse the Allegheny Mountains to get to Pittsburgh and further west. In 1844-45, he designed his first suspension bridge, in addition to building four suspension bridge aqueducts. He also filled the need for wrought iron entrances to residences and stores.

In 1850, Abraham Hewitt, owner of the Cooper-Hewitt Iron Company, convinced Roebling to move to Trenton to provide iron and steel at a good price. In the 1850's, Roebling designed a suspension bridge over the Niagara Gorge and the Wheeling Bridge linking West Virginia and Ohio. Still improving his steel cable techniques, he undertook the Niagara Falls Bridge and the Cincinnati Bridge.

The iconic Brooklyn Bridge (1869-1883) became his signature construction, the longest suspension bridge of its time. In an age when American bridges regularly collapsed, The Roebling Steel and Iron Company built more than 30-bridges, all of which stood the test of time.

By 1870, the Roebling Company manufactured seven hundred tons of wire rope with eighty-five employees. As the hungry market for consumer goods increased, so did Roebling's enterprise.[1]

A Trenton game, quoits (circular rings), became more popular rather than horseshoes because the backyards were smaller in Trenton and Trenton made an abundance of steel.

The pottery industry began in 1669. Trenton's sixty-two potteries employed a large workforce that initially manufactured earthenware but later specialized in sanitary pottery for indoor plumbing.

By 1854, Trenton had a population of 6,000. Denbar and Schenck began to manufacture rubber. Eventually, the giant company, Goodyear Rubber, bought the company to begin a towering industry. Joining Denbar and Schenck in manufacturing rubber were what became prominent Trenton families, such as, Stokes, Maddox, Sickel, Skirm, Haverstick, Linburg, Oliphant, Lowthrop, Dickinson, Bell and Vannest.[2]

Other manufacturers included The New Jersey School Furniture Company., the Fitzgibbon & Crisp Company, and makers of automobile bodies. The garment industry developed manufacturing, such as the Strauss worsted and silk mills, and the Princeton Worsted Mills.

Manufacturing became king in this small town making watches. refrigerators, lamps, tools, cigars, zinc, swords, beds and mattresses, paper mills and paper bags (both residential and commercial) and its famous Old Trenton Crackers.

Griffith Electric and Tab Electric companies distributed more than 15,000 items. During WWII, General Motors' Fisher Body plant near Trenton converted to making aircraft. Griffith became a very successful industrial electrical supplier.

Figure 3. Alexander Rubber Company

Consumer Society

Good marketing is selling the right product at the right time at the right price. After World War 1, the American economy turned from an industrial to a consumer economy. Telephones, electricity, convenience appliances, ready-to-wear clothing as well as consumer credit swept the nation. The automobile industry provided an enormous stimulus for the national economy. Trenton manufacturing capitalized on its manufacturing prowess. In Trenton, Jewish merchants became an important link between increased manufacturing and the increasing consumer needs of its workers.

Victor Lebow in *Price Competition (1955) stated:*

"Our enormously productive economy . . . demands that we make consumption our way of life that we convert the buying and use of

goods into rituals, that we seek our spiritual satisfaction, our ego satisfaction, in consumption...we need things consumed, burned up, replaced and discarded at an ever-accelerating rate." [3]

TRENTON'S JEWS – THE FIRST JEWISH IMMIGRANTS TO THE UNITED STATES

Trenton's Jews followed a normal pattern of three waves of Jewish immigration; the Sephardic Jews (fleeing from the Spanish Inquisition) in Revolutionary War days; the German Jews, 1820-1880; and the Russian and Eastern European Jews, 1881-1914. The causation of these waves of Jewish immigration makes for fascinating reading. Accordingly, after Trenton's Jews are covered, a more detailed explanation of the immigration waves is discussed subsequently.

The First Jewish Immigrants to Trenton

The first recorded entry of Jewish involvement in Trenton was Philadelphian Simon Gratz who bought shares in the Trenton Banking Company in 1805. (Gratz was the little known son of Bernard Gratz of Silesia, settling in Philadelphia in 1759 establishing many Jewish institutions, including congregation, Mikveh Israel. Simon was one of the founders of the Pennsylvania Academy of Fine Arts. He also was treasurer of the Mikveh Israel in the 1820's.) [4]

Rabbi S. Joshua Kohn, writing in the 1964 American Jewish Historical Quarterly found that, in 1839, Dr. Daniel Levy Maduro Peixotto, of New York City became co-editor of Trenton's *Emporium and True American*. He also practiced medicine in New York. In 1853, David Naar, a brother-in-law of Dr. Peixotto, bought the newspaper, now called *The Daily True American*. Living outside of Elizabeth, New Jersey (Wheatsheaf,), and the populace elected him as a lay Judge in the Common Pleas Court of Essex County. He used the appellation 'Judge' thereafter.

Naar's family traced its origins to Jewish expulsion from Portugal in 1497; to Amsterdam; to St. Thomas in the Caribbean; to New York in the 1750's.

David Naar became an influential Democrat through his editorial stances in the *Trenton True American*. He had served as a delegate in the 1844 State Constitutional Convention where he made sure that there were no restrictions to elected office precluded by religion as well as well as introducing Bill of Rights. [5] David Naar played a very important part in the civic and cultural life of Trenton, in the political life of New Jersey, and in national politics as a staunch Democrat. As owner and editor of the *Daily True American*, he became a spokesperson of the Democratic Party in New Jersey. He edited the newspaper for more than half a century, from 1853 to 1905. His nephew, Moses D. Naar, and by David's son, Joseph L. Naar continued until the *True American* went out of business. In 1908, a son of Joseph L. Naar, Henry Kelsey Naar, became treasurer of the newspaper.

President James K. Polk appointed Naar as Commercial Agent of the United States to St. Thomas on June 19, 1845. Thereafter, he returned to Wheatsheaf where he was elected Recorder of the Borough and a member of the Borough Council. In 1851-1852, the N.J. General Assembly appointed him as their clerk.[6]

In Trenton, Judge Naar busied himself in his newly adopted city by advocating better teacher education, (realized in 1855 with the State Normal School located in Trenton) and adequate libraries. Indeed, the voters elected him to the Trenton Common Council in 1869-70. In 1871, he became President of the City Council. He also served as President of Trenton's Board of Education for 1854-1855, 1861-1862, and 1866-1868.

David Naar died on February 24, 1880. The Reverend Dr. Henry Pereira Mendes of New York and the Reverend George Jacobs of Philadelphia officiated at religious services held at his home (146 West State Street) in Trenton.

Figure 4. Naar's Trenton True American Newspaper Building

Among the pallbearers there was one identifiable Jewish name—Abraham Lowenstein. David Naar, was buried in the family plot in Evergreen Cemetery, outside of Elizabeth, NJ. Judger Naar's nephews and son, however were buried in Har Saini's cemetery. It should be added, that there were twelve Naar burials at Har Sinai's cemetery at Vroom and Liberty Streets in Trenton and the Har Sinai Section of the Greenwood Cemetery in Trenton. In the 1890's, Har Sinai Temple's cemetery merged with Congregation Brothers of Israel.[7]

Devin Naar, a Rutgers professor, traced his family genealogy, typical of refugees of the Spanish-Portuguese Inquisition. [8]

The Naar's located to Dutch controlled St. Thomas Island where Judge David Naar was born. [9]

Trenton Times historian, Harry Podmore, reported David Naar's fiftieth wedding anniversary celebration in 1870. He mentioned the genealogical tree of the Naar's, dating 'back to the time of the discovery of America by Columbus.'[10]

German Jews Arrive in Trenton, 1840-1880

In the late 1840's German Jews came in dribbles to Trenton. By 1857, there were a sufficient number to establish the Har Sinai Cemetery Association. In 1858, the Jews of Trenton organized Har Sinai Hebrew Congregation. Although not particularly observant, Judge Naar became a founding member of Har Sinai Hebrew Congregation and spoke at its opening ceremony in 1857.

German Jewish Arrivals in Trenton

German Jews settled in Trenton in the 1840s. Products of the Enlightenment, the most prominent among them was Simon Kahnweiler, a merchant and manufacturer. His brothers, Leon and Emanuel followed shortly thereafter. [11]

Sidney Goldmann wrote that the 1840s bought additional German Jewish families to the area: Dannenburg, Kahn, Schoninger, Frank and Mankos. In the 1850's some of families were: families: Goldberg, Rosenblatt, Samler, Weinberg, Lowenstein, Solomon, Bohn, among others. [12]

Figure 5. Har Sinai's First Jewish Cemetery
(Shared 30 years later with Brothers of Israel)

Joseph Rice was the first recorded German Jew to arrive in Trenton in 1857. He operated a store for fifty years at 212 Academy Street. He became a trustee at Mechanics Bank as well as a trustee to the State Hospital. He also served on the Trenton Water Board and Fire Board.

Bespeaking Joseph Rice's high business leadership and citizenship is his obituary appearing in the Trenton Evening Times, of July 15, 1913.

> *Joseph Rice Dies at Belmar Home*
>
> *One of Trenton's Pioneer Merchants and Long a Faithful Public Official*
>
> *After having been in impaired health several years, Joseph Rice of this city, died yesterday afternoon at his summer residence in Belmar. His children were present when the, end came. They are Mrs. Abe Siegel and Mrs. Lewis A. Fuld of this city; Mrs. B. Straus of Newark and Alexander S. Rice, of the Electric Specialty Company. His eldest son, Jonas D. Rice died a short time ago.*
>
> *Mr. Rice was one of Trenton's eldest and most highly regarded citizens. He had been a member of the board of managers of the State Hospital [for the insane] in this city, and official of the Mechanics National Bank. Many years ago he began the clothing business here,*

10

succeeded by the Rice Clothing Comp any, under which name his son took over the business . . .

In the building of Taylor Opera House, in 1866, Mr. Rice was a leading spirit and had always been a member of its Board of Directors. He was also one of the oldest members of the Masonic fraternity in the city. For fifty years, Rice resided at 221 Academy Street . . . He spent the summers at his home at Belmar as one of the early settlers.

For fifteen years, he served on the Trenton Water Board and was also a member of the Fire Board for six' years. Mr. Rice was one of the pioneers in the clothing trade here. Before he went into business for himself, he was employed as a clerk by Isaac Wyman, who conducted a clothing store on Warren Street, near Front [Street], later in a building on the site now occupied by the First National Bank, on State Street, west of Broad Street. Mr. Rice's first store in 1857 was in the building just below the Trenton Bank . . .A few years later moved to Broad Street, above the City Hall.[13]

Other German settlers and business leaders included the Wyman family, led by Albert who operated clothing stores that served as training ground for future clothiers, including Joseph Rice.

Abraham Lowenstein, a brother-in-law of Wyman, was a clothier on Broad St, near Dunham's, then adjacent to First Presbyterian Church on State St. (Remember, City Hall was located on the site that became Dunham's until the 1920's.) His son, Isaac Lowenstein, succeeded him as a successful businessman. He also was an excellent violinist. Meyer Cohen, from Lambertville, was Trenton's haberdasher. His store located in the Lincoln Building on State and Broad Sts. When he died, he left a fortune to his son, Louis, who greatly expanded the business.

Other clothiers were Marcus Bohn and Simon Kahnweller. Kahnweiler started out as a brick manufacturer. Then, he became a clothing merchant on North Warren St. He became wealthy in the Civil War by supplying substitute soldiers for those who paid him a sum of money. Kahnweiler also had a brother-in-law, Mr. Marks who operated a clothing store on State and Warren Sts.

David Manco operated a store on East State St near the old city hall. Simeon Samler, the Washington Market Clothing store on Broad St, near Front St., near the Philadelphia Bargain store owned by Henry Wirtshafter. Samler's son, David succeeded him.

In 1878, Sam Grumbacher opened a dry goods store. His brother, Jacob owned a wholesale tobacco operation on North Broad St. Another son, Max ran a chain of department stores. Sam Gumbacher was the first Jewish elected official, serving on the City Council.

Other German Jewish merchants were Sigmund Keehn, the Washington Market hatter, Louis Cohen, another hatter, and B. Fabian. D. Block was manager of the Washington - Market Clothing Company. Morris May retired in 1897 from the jewelry business in 1897.

Still others were L. Simon, operating a wool business with Lirburg, Stoke & CO., and Abe Belga, who owned a clothing furnishings store.

Louis Fuld, a famous Trenton name, and a relative of Joseph Rice, owned the Comfort shoe store. In the next generation, Felix Fuld became a philanthropist donating more than one million dollars, including the Y.M.H.A.

Other German Jewish merchants were D. Gundling (jeweler). Moses Wormsen (clothier), Mr. Ginsberg, (garment manufacturer), D. Plough (fruit and produce), Mr. Plough also was part proprietor of Lehman & Co.'s Newark Cash Grocery, Samuel Levy (Cigar Factory), S. Papier (clothier), David Newton (Dry Cleaner and Dyer), Mr. Stearns managed the Rothschild's shirt factory.

A 1901 edition of the Trenton Times announced that Dr. Nathan Stern, Har Sinai's Reform Rabbi, spoke of Thanksgiving as an American Jewish Day of celebration. Dr. Nathan Stern, a Har Sinai's Reform Jewish Rabbi proclaimed that Thanksgiving is a holiday to be celebrated by American Jews giving thanks for its freedom and opportunity.

Dr. S. Ettinger (1801-1856) in his 1840's portrayed several Polish and Galician Jewish immigrants returning to Europe, for the purpose of marrying a Jewish women Nonetheless, contact between Trenton and Germany appeared to be very superficial, which may indicate that return to Europe was small.[14]

Even in the early days of Trenton's industrialization, Jewish storeowners and peddlers avoided competition with others in the industrial job market. Wholesaling and retailing split along ethnic lines. The more capital-intensive wholesaling sector was dominated by native whites along with a few Jews, all of them male. In contrast, retailing remained much more open to diverse groups such as Jews.

Although Trenton's Har Sinai did not formally join the Reform movement until 1922, it employed graduates of the Reform Seminary and adopted many of its American-Jewish practices.[15]

In 1856, the *Trenton State Gazette* newspaper reported Har Sinai's hosting a Passover celebration.

Figure 6. Miss Liberty Receiving Jewish Immigrants

In 1860, members began permanent services. They held meetings in the old Chancery Building (West State Street and Chancery Lane). At a meeting held on July 22, 1860, the congregation decided formally to incorporate and the following elected trustees: Simon Kahnweiler, Isaac Wymann, Henry Shoninger, Herman Rosenbaum, Marcus Aaron, L. Kahnweiler and David Manko. For many years members conducted services in German and Hebrew only.

In 1865, Simon Kahnweiler, the first president, purchased a small Lutheran chapel on North Montgomery Street in downtown Trenton. In 1866, dedication ceremonies featured the Rabbi D. Frankel, of Philadelphia, Rabbi Isaiah Gotz and Rabbi Reuben Straus. Judge David Naar delivered the dedicatory address. Rabbi Isaac Lesser, a liberal traditional Rabbi, who would later become the founder of the Jewish Conservative Movement and Rev. Jacob Frankel, a Jewish Chaplin appointed by Pres. Lincoln, also attended. The congregation adopted Protestant practices and education techniques (Sunday schools, hospitals, the religious press, charitable societies, and the like) in order to strengthen Judaism in the face of pressures upon Jews to convert.

In 1872, due to a flaw in Har Sinai's deed, the real estate re-sold at a Sheriff's auction. Nonetheless, Mrs. Toretta Kaufman, mother of S. E. Kaufman, convened a fund to re-purchase. Joseph Rice made up the balance needed.

In 1877, these Jews founded Chevra Bikkur Cholim (Society for the Sick), "for the mutual relief of the sick and the burial of the dead," following a Jewish practice to provide for its weakest and most vulnerable members.

In 1903, the congregation moved to the G.A.R. (Grand Army of the Republic) building on Montgomery St. Their next location in 1904 was at corner of Front and Stockton Streets. Its officers were Sigmund Baron, president; Abraham Siegle, vice-president; Louis Cohen, treasurer; and Jonas D. Rice, secretary. [16]

We will resume an account of this congregation when we discuss all Jewish congregation.

Figure 7. Jews in Cracow, Poland

14

Russian Jews Arrive, 1881-1914

A 1902, a Trenton newspaper account indicates that Isaac Goodstein was the first of the Russian Jew to locate in Trenton, in 1875. When he realized the possibilities for Jews, he encouraged Wolf Fineberg to immigrate. Not long after, he sent for his brother, Abe Bernstein. They all located on East Front Street, near Warren to begin business as peddlers. When they made enough money, they opened up their stores. Isaac Goldstein became a superintendent of a new silk waist company on Donnelly's alley.

Goldstein indicated that as Trenton's Jewish population increased, at least one-half settled in South Trenton, displacing the resident Irish population on Union, Fall, Decatur, Warren and Market Streets. [17]

In 1881, Jacob Barker came to Trenton with his wife and seven children. Another newcomer, Meyer Stark, arrived in 1883 to tutor five German families in religious instruction.[18] Abraham Levy, another early settler in 1886 took the same route as Meyer Stark by starting out Russia (Lithuania), living in Scotland and then coming to Trenton. [19]

Figure 8. Peddling Cart

Figure 9. English as a Second Language in Yiddish

Trenton's Jewish Immigrant Community – South Trenton

In 1888, Joseph Movshovich opened the first bank on Decatur St. There were twelve kosher butchers. In 1895, Harry Alexander opened the first kosher deli. Alex Cohen was a boxing promoter and cut man.

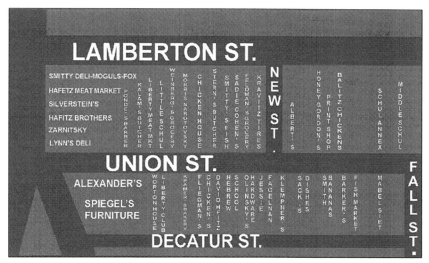

Figure 10. South Trenton Map

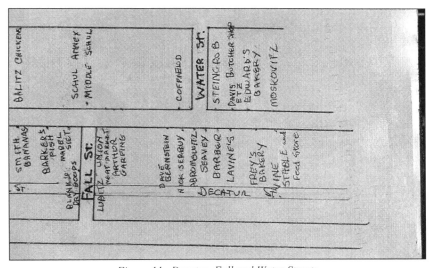

Figure 11. Decatur, Fall and Water Streets

Other early South Trenton residents included Isaac Berman, Solomon Goldstein, David Lavine, Max Feinberg, Harry Haveson, Israel Silverstein, Isaac Levy, Israel Kohn, Gabriel Lavinson, Louis Levy, Solomon Urken, Daniel Levine and Abraham Moskowitz.

On commercial Market Street situated three Deli's; a Drug Store; a Restaurants; 3-Bakers; a Gas Station, a Dentist (Dr. Bloom); 3-Butchers; a Furniture store; a Mikveh (Religious Ritual Bath). On Union St., we counted: 3-Shuls; a Hotel; a Social Club (Liberty Club); 3- Bakeries; 2-Chicken stores; 2-Fish Markets; 5-Butchers; a Hardware store; 3-Dry Goods Stores; a Tire Store; a Clothing ship; and a Print shop.

The aggregate totals were 6-bakers, 8-butchers, 3 dry goods stores; 3-Deli's, 3- Dry Goods Stores, 3-shuks, 2 Fish stores, 2-chicken stores. We found one Mikveh (Ritual Bath), Hotel, a saddle shop, a cooperage (barrels) Restaurant, Gas station, Tire Store, Print shop, Hardware store, barber and social club. For a further information, see Appendix 1.

South Trenton produced numerous professionals (physicians, lawyers, accountants, dentists, etc.), business people and other earnest citizens. Not bad for a people who fled the oppression of Russia with little or nothing to invest.

Judge Mark Litowitz embellished this walk down memory Lane. He related that his favorites were Fox's Deli, the Starr Bakery. Litowitz' Uncle Sam owned S. Litowitz and Sons, fruit and produce dealers. Along with their father, the three Litowitz sons (Harry, Deckie and Lou), operated the successful enterprise on Tucker St.

The Mikveh (Jewish ritual bath) stood at the corner of Market and Mill Sts. at the apex of the convergence of a triangular intersection. Going towards the river, there was a tinsmith, the Litowitz residence, and a shoe repair shop.

Kohn's Deli was known for its corn rye breads; Kunes' for its sweets. Popkin's gas station occupied Market and Union Sts. servicedthe new automobile drivers that swept the area in the 1920's. The Liberty Club, known as the 'Kachunkie', an institution, for gin and poker card players. Poker occasionally meant big-stake gambling. The Club initially was on Lamberton St., cared for by Rufus Popkin.

Judge Litowitz describes South Trenton as place where one could feel secure. Everyone knew each other and looked out for each other. No one got in serious trouble – the neighbors saw to that. If there was a ruckus, the 'mob boss,' married to a Jewish woman, took care of business.

Love and trust transcended race, creed, and gender. The sharing was incredible. No locks on any house door! Immigrant parents emphasized education (as the Trenton High School Yearbook shows from 1922-37 shows). Education, indigenous to Jewish culture, was the ticket to become successful in America.

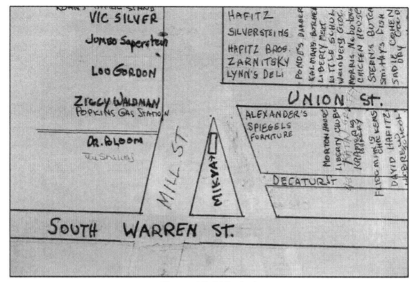

Figure 12. Mikveh Area

South Trenton produced numerous professionals (physicians, lawyers, accountants, dentists, etc.), business people and solid citizens. Not bad for a people who fled the oppression of Russia with little or nothing to invest.

In 1917, approximately 7,100 Jews (6%) inhabited Trenton. Most of this population resided in the area between South Broad and Warren streets, and Market Street and the Delaware-Raritan Canal (Now the Trenton Freeway). [20]

The South Trenton area benefitted from the general improving infrastructure of a growing industrial Trenton. South Trenton benefitted from trolley service along Broad St, sidewalks, potable water (1859) and sewerage (beginning in 1903 but not completed until 1923) and outdoor lighting.

Further, in the early 1900's, most houses had modern plumbing of hot and cold running water, indoor plumbing with its toilet, bathtub and wash area, and electricity. Further, it had bright electric streetlights in 1887 (Its first electric lights made their Trenton appearance in 1881)[21] The City Railway South Broad Street, bordering what was to become the Hungarian Jewish area.

Further, the City Railway Company extended its line from Perry Street to Warren and then to Ferry Street, up Bridge and into Centre Street down as far as Riverview Cemetery.

To facilitate transportation of goods and of passengers to Philadelphia and New York, the Pennsylvania Railroad was three blocks away.

Ozzie Zuckerman reported that in early Jewish Trenton many Jews became peddlers because they could celebrate the Sabbath without business pressures. Others were junkyard dealers for the same reason. In the early days, in fact, there existed a Sabbath silence in South Trenton because all the stores closed.

Several news articles told of the government's prosecution against merchants who closed on the Jewish Sabbath (Saturdays) but opened on Sundays, against the Blue Laws, prohibiting conducting business on the Christian Sabbath. Articles in the Trenton Times record those prominent and not so prominent merchants who were cited. The Jewish community leaders resolved this issue by political favors. Nonetheless, businesses reopened on Sunday with the wink and the nod of the Police Department.

Peddlers earned about five dollars a week and rarely grossed a profit, often depending on the wives and children to peddle alongside of them. The peddler lifestyle marked a profound loss of status for many of the immigrants.[22]

To round out the cultural connectedness of Trenton's Jewish community, it published two Yiddish newspapers 1909 and 1916. [23]

Newly arrived Jews experienced profound culture shock. The new American workday was no longer circumscribed by meals shared with family, prayer, or Jewish holidays and the Sabbath. Many Jews agonized over the abandonment of their structured   religious traditions of their homogenous shtetl life.

Since the Russian government, with few exceptions, prevented Jews from owning land or raw materials, Eastern European Jews possessed a skill set different from other immigrants. With some exceptions for those in the cities, the Eastern European Jewish immigrants possessed skills as merchants from the Russian shtetls.[24]

Experiencing merchandising in Odessa, The five Finkle brothers became door-to-door peddlers traversing a weekly route from Trenton to Lambertville, to Flemington, to Somerville back to Trenton for the Sabbath selling their wares to both farmers and small townsmen. When one earned sufficient money, he sent for the second brother ad seriatim. Eventually, with enough capital, they settled in Trenton and environs to establish dry goods stores. In Lambertville, Finkle's Hardware Store still operates, more than 110 years later.

Figure 13. Russian Jewish Immigrant in New York

Life in South Trenton was far from easy. Representing the least expensive properties in the city, infrastructure facilities such as sewer, water, street lights, electricity and street cars were slow to arrive as well as other municipal services. Then there was the disorganization of a new urban area, with cattle running amok, street car deaths and serious injuries.

Medically, in addition to untreated infection complications, there were the communicable diseases that today are eliminated through immunization procedures (DPT shots, etc.). Communicable diseases easily passed from child to child in schools and play-yards. Medical science had not evolved to treat communicable diseases and only the rich had access to medical care. Communicable diseases included Chicken Pox: Pink eye (Conjunctivitis), Polio, Influenza (flu), hand, mouth and foot disease, head lice, hepatitis A, measles, meningitis, mumps, whooping cough (pertussis), ringworm, rotavirus and scabies, among others.

Active in the religious life of the Orthodox congregations were: the Rev. P. Turman, the Rev. Mr. Prail, the Rev. Max Sufnuss, the Rev. Meyer Rabinowitz, the Rev. Israel Price, Rabbi Isaac Bunin, the Rev. Joseph Konvitz, David Lavine, Isaac Levy (Levie), a founder of the Talmud Torah, Hyman Levy (Levie), first president of the congregation of the Brothers of Israel, Max Gordon and Rabbi Issachar Levin.

By 1907, Trenton Jews numbered approximately 4,000 souls. Discounting 700 German Jews and 250 Hungarian Jews, left with 3,050 Russian Jews. If there were seven to family, then there would have been 435 Russian Jewish families in Trenton.

The unique feature of Trenton is its small Jewish community of approximately 400-450. Because second generation Jews married other Jews who generally lived in Trenton, the incidence of relatedness by blood or by marriage is enormous.

For example, if a family of eight children all married, then eight other families would be related, totaling nine (including the original family). Multiply that result by 400 and one concludes that most Jews are related to one another in this small Trenton Jewish community. [25]

Perhaps a non-Jewish resident of the area, Mike Kuzma, summed it up:

The "Jewtown" [his designation] I recall, began at Market and Broad where Market St. began its descent into the Valley of the Israelites" as Harry Berkowitz described it. It extended to the [Delaware] river. From Market St. it extended South to Bridge St. and encompassed all the streets in between; Cooper, Lamberton, Union, Mill, Decatur, Fall, New, (no not "Nu") and Water Streets.

Beyond the big Shul [Congregtion People of Truth] was Steingrob's Grocery Store with the huge peanut roaster in the window. Two doors down was Edward's bakery (who could forget "Fran") directly across Union St. was Frey's Bakery, and Lavine's Dept. Store run by Sam, who was the consummate merchant. The short 200 block of Fall St. had yet another fine bakery; Feldman's on the corner of Decatur.

Directly across was Sada Hannah's (Mrs. Blank) dry goods and notion store. Other merchant's on this block were Barney Horowitz butcher, Jules Leahman butcher and often bookmaker, a fruit/produce stand, Arthur Finklestein's United Meat market, where Arthur always offered me a fresh hot dog to nosh on when shopping with my Mom. On the corner across from the big Shul was the Union meat market run by the Millner's, who along with Jake Daner owned the Delaware Packing Co. just two blocks west on Fall and Bloomsbury St. across from Scmulkie Berger . . . a "Cattle Dealer"

Just beyond Bloomsbury St. at the River was Sokalner Brother's Hide's and Skins. My dad worked for this wonderful family for 40 years, and they were like family to us. Some of my siblings, including myself, were named after members of their family.

Warren St. had "Tomar's Department Store", Bobby Binder's Electrical supply, Urken's hardware, Stan Stern's mish mash shop of 'chochkelas.' [cheap products].

Peddlers situated near the "Horsenally" situated next to the Princeton Worsted Mills on Bloomsbury St., to the River. The peddlers with horse drawn carts housed their mighty steeds each night. We kids would sneak in after dark, take the horses out, and ride like Gene Autry, and Roy Rogers along the grassy strip beside the Delaware River.

"Ben's Deli" on the corner of Lamberton and Market . . . was the reason business bustled in Jewtown. People for miles would travel to our little enclave by the river to enjoy the best-corned beef this side of NYC.

Of course, this is not what I told Alex Segal [Director of 'Playhouse 90' fame] and whose father had the deli a few doors up on Market St. next to Kohn's bakery. During a casting call for an Alex Segal movie made in Trenton, I yelled out that his father had the best Pastrami in Town ...got me a two line-speaking role in his film "Some Most Honorable Men" starring Van Heflin, and Peter Fonda.

Today, the area is no more, a victim of urban renewal in the early 1960's.[26] Sherry Speizle rhapsodized: "Being from Lakewood, which was a small, sleepy town in those days, I considered Trenton to be the big city," she continued. "There were department stores and restaurants. I remember getting dressed up on Saturday nights to go to the movies. It was a time when Trenton was a true destination." Said Herb Spiegel:

"My dad came to Trenton with 20-bucks in his pocket. He eventually brought a garage on Market Street. Years later, he bought the whole building, which once had been my grandfather's hotel, lost during the Depression. My Dad was thrilled to bring the property back to our family. Ernie Kovacs performed the first commercials for our store. Willie Mays used to come to the store. And, of course, there were the locals."

"It was such a vibrant area," said Spiegel. "Everyone had a favorite deli or butcher shop. So many people from my generation married their high school sweetheart and went into the family business. That's just the way it was. The next generation in large part didn't stay in the area. It's heart-wrenching to see what happened to this once-lovely city. [27]

Larry Greenfield spoke of a Trenton Icon, Greenfield's Luncheonette. State and Clinton. Across from the old YMCA and the nearby Rider Business School, just down the block from the train station. Willie Mays and Ernie Kovacs used to patronize the store. . Half of Rider College used to hang out there. Moe and Trudy Greenfield were my grandparents, still remembered fondly by such esteemed Trentonians as Arnie and Bertha Ropeik.[28]

From another Kosher butcher's granddaughter, Phyllis Stern, shared this photograph:

Figure 14. Stern's Kosher Meat Market

24

Figure 15. Hayfetz Kosher Meats

Edith Heyfetz Gordon showed her families Kosher Butcher shop. Estelle Rabstein Bogad reminisced:

I was raised in Trenton until 1946. , at which date I married Milt Bogad. I lived on Perry Street. I did not live in any Jewish section because my Dad first had a soda factory and when prohibition was repealed, we had a liquor store at that location.

I had two sisters, one was Ruth Rabstein Pellettieri, who defended the "Trenton Six" My other sister was Rose Rabstein Hirsch who was married to Sam Hirsch. I graduated from Trenton High School in "39, graduated Temple University in "43, and taught at Trenton High "from "43 to "46.

I wanted to fill you in on Trenton before the 40"s. There were three shuls [synagogues] on Union Street. The first one from Market Street was one of the smallest [Anshei Fife – Workers of Truth] and one of the poorest. My family was a member there forever. My Dad was responsible for building the house for Rabbi Kantorowitz.

To give you more on Trenton - the BEST Jewish bakery on Market Street was Kohn's. Mae Kohn, one of the daughters, ran it for years. [The Kunis Bakery owners may disagree]. A dairy store was on the corner of Market and Cooper. Coming toward Union you had Siegel's Deli. You haven't eaten deli until you had it from there.

We all went to the Y. We had a Girl's social club that met there. Our senior advisor was Edith Citroen. What fun!!! Name of the club was Cleophas Club.

Trenton's first-generation of Russian Jewish immigrants struggled to adapt to American (secular) norms. The second generation, rejected their parents' 'otherness' and normalized themselves in a secular society, generally retaining their Jewish cultural heritage.

After World War II, Jews perceived Jewish birth as a matter of course, even if they did not prize it. Neither did they engender negative attitudes towards Judaism. The relationship was best characterized as indifferent.

Trenton's Jewish Surnames

The 1921 Trenton City Directory revealed 118 Jewish Surnames (some, like Smith and Brown are assumed to be Jewish).[29] See Appendix 4. Jewish Surnames.

Trenton's Jewish Publications

In addition to the two short-lived Yiddish newspapers, Trenton produced *The Trenton Jewish World* (Budson, Miller and Firestein, 1909), and The Trenton Jewish Weekly (H. Waxler, 1916), both of which lasted of short duration. Readership of New York's large Yiddish papers: *The Forverts* (Socialist; now *The Jewish Daily Forward*, the *Tageblaatt* (Orthodox religious), *La America* (Ladino), *Dos Abend Blatt* (Workers view; an outgrowth of the weekly *Di Arbeter Tsaytung*), *Der Blatt* (Satmar Hasidim), Freie Arbeiter Stimme (The Free Voice of Labor) was the longest-running anarchist periodical in the Yiddish language), *Der Groyser Kundes* (Satarist), *Jewish Morning Journal* (A politically conservative, Orthodox Jewish) and the *Morgen Freiheit* (Morning Freedom - Communist).

In 1919, with the backing of the Y.M.H.A. and Y.W.H.A., several secular clubs and events occurred. In 1924, Dr. M. H. Chaseman established the magazine to increase Jewish literary. The *Messenger's* first literary contest in 1925 awarded prizes to Max Litt (first); Charles Lavinthal (Second) and Max Pitasky (third).

Its next editor, I. Herbert Levy, brought many local writers to fill the pages with interesting news of the Trenton Jewish Community. Some of these reporters were Percy Seietlin, Nathan Kramer, Abraham Adler, Albert H. Kahn, Rabbi Holzberg, Herman Babitch, Sidney Lavine and Lillian Berdow.

In 1928, Sidney Goldmann (later to be State Archivist and Superior Court Judge), was the next editor-in-chief to configure the *Community Messenger* as a viable magazine. In collaboration with the "Y," Max Lehman (later to become an aide the New York's Mayor) was poetry editor; Julian Goodstein (excellent musician and haberdasher) was fine arts editor and Julius Schey was an art critic.[30]

Early Jewish Civic Leaders

Many of Har Sinai's German Jews were merchants. Among them was the already mentioned Simon Kahnweiler. He became the first Jewish manufacturer (bricks). His brother, Emanuel, operated a soap factory near the Assunpink Bridge on South Broad Street.

S. E. Kaufman, for many years the proprietor of the Kaufman department store, lived in Trenton. He was one of the leaders of Trenton's Board of Trade (now Chamber of Commerce). He became a member of the Interstate Bridge Commission and the executive board of the Boy Scouts of America.

Albert Wyman, another early arrival, operated clothing stores, serving as a training ground for future clothiers, including Joseph Rice. Abraham Lowenstein, a brother-in law of Wyman, was a clothier on Broad St, near Dunham's, then adjacent to First Presbyterian Church on State St. (Remember, City Hall was located on the site that became Dunham's until the 1920's.)

Joseph Rice became a successful clothier, leaving the business to his sons, Alexander and Jonas. Rice also became Director of the Mechanics National Bank. Henry Wirtschafter maintained a large department store on South Broad Street.

Abraham Lowenstein, a Brother- in-law of Wyman, operated a Clothing store on Broad St, near Dunham's, then adjacent to First Presbyterian Church on State St. (Remember, City Hall located on the site that became Dunham's in the

1920's). His son, Isaac Lowenstein, succeeded him as a successful businessman.) He also was an excellent violinist.)

Meyer Cohen was Trenton's haberdasher. His store located in the Lincoln Building on State and Broad Sts. When he died, he left a fortune to his son, Louis, who greatly expanded the business. Other clothiers were Marcus Bohn and Simon Kahnweller. Kahnweiler started out as a brick manufacturer. Then, he became a clothing merchant on North Warren St. He became wealthy in the Civil War by supplying substitute soldiers for recompense. Kahnweiler also had a brother-in-law, Mr. Marks who operated a clothing store on State and Warren Sts.

David Manco operated a store on East State St near the old city hall. Simeon Samler, the Washington Market Clothing store on Broad St, near Front St., near the Philadelphia Bargain store owned by Henry Wirtshafter. Samler's son, David succeeded him.

Sam Grumbacher in 1878, opened a dry goods store. His brother, Jacob owned a wholesale tobacco operation on North Broad St. Another son, Max operated a chain of department stores.

Other German Jewish merchants were Sigmund Keehn, the Washington Market hatter, Louis Cohen, another hatter, and B. Fabian. D. Block was manager of the Washington - Market Clothing Company. Morris May, a jeweler, retired in 1897.

Still others were L. Simon, operating a wool business of Lirburg, Stoke & CO., and Abe Belga, who owned a clothing furnishings store.

Louis Fuld, a famous Trenton name, and a relative of Joseph Rice, owned the Comfort shoe store. M. A. Fuld owned a shoe store In the State Gazette building. In the next generation, Felix Fuld became a philanthropist donating more than one million dollars, including the Y.M.H.A.

Other German Jewish merchants were D. Gundling (jeweler). Moses Wormsen (clothier), Mr. Ginsberg, (garment manufacturer), D. Plough (fruit and produce), Mr. Plough also was part proprietor of Lehman & Co.'s Newark Cash Grocery, Samuel Levy (Cigar Factory), S. Papier (clothier), David Newton (Dry Cleaner and Dyer), Mr. Stearns managed the Rothschild's shirt factory.

A 1901 edition of the Trenton Times announced that Dr. Nathan Stern, Har Sinai's Reform Rabbi, spoke of Thanksgiving as an American Jewish Day of celebration.

Sam Gumbacher was the first Jewish elected official, serving on the City Council.

Trenton's Jewish Benevolent and Religious Institutions

Jewish communities provided for the orphan and widow. Indeed, Deuteronomy 26:12 declares, "The underprivileged to which the poor man's tithe was to be given includes the orphan, and the widow." Exodus 22:21-3 states emphatically: "If you do mistreat them [widow and orphan], I will heed their cry as soon as they cry out to Me, and My anger shall blaze forth and I will put you to the sword, and your own wives shall become widows and your children orphans).

Established firmly in the Jewish Code of Law, (1565), Trenton's Jews created and maintained its commitment to the vulnerable. Beginning in 1877, Trentonians created the Bikur Cholim Society to help the sick and to bury the dead. In succession, more associations followed - the Har Sinai Charity Society (1893), Hebrew Benevolent Society (1894), Trenton Hebrew Benevolent Society (1895) and the Hebrew Charitable Association of Trenton (1908), which became the Hebrew Free Loan Society (1930).

The Ladies Sick benefit society (1909) provided food, clothing shelter and small sums of money. Its incorporators were: Fanny Budson, Judge Philip Forman, Rose Golinsky, Louis Rudner and Florence Vogel.

Ultimately, voluntary groups to help families institutionalized in 1927, becoming the Jewish Family Welfare Board, the Jewish Family Service and a Home for the Aged and Infirm. In that year, Director Ms. Galinsky reported that the agency assisted 66 families, with 1,150 food orders, 28 tons of coal and clothing for more than 100 children. Louis Rudner was its first President.

The Bureau significantly helped those uprooted by the German troubles on the 1930's. To relocate those German Jews lucky to escape their impending doom in the 1930's, the agency materially helped 44-families adapt to a strange environment during an anxious time. After the war, the Bureau helped numerous refugees (Displaced Persons) find a residence, a job and special services in order to adapt to their new environment.

People who worked on these projects were Claire Kind, Jessica Alexander, Dr. Samuel Blaugrun, Joseph Fishberg, Rose Galinsky, Sidney Goldman, Fanny Popkin, Sol Walkoff, Reba Byer, Sadie Shalita and Rose Feber Baker, Mildred Forer, Katherine Papier Freida Garber, Fannie Kohn, May Medoff, Beulah Glickman and Fay Schragger. Harold Hoenig and Harry Holland.

Its Executive Directors were: David E. Tannebaum,, Jerome Palevsky (1956-70), Byron Pinsky (1970-73), Leo M. Kalik, and Linda Meisel.

Presidents of the Jewish Welfare Board: Louis Rudner, Sidney S. Stark, Sidney Goldman, Samuel Leventhal, Leon Robinson, Maurice Ross, Philip J. Albert, David Kravitz, Marvin Swern, Harry Holland, Maurice G. Kott, Max Bard, Harold Koslow, and Harold Hoenig and Saul Gillman.

Renamed the Jewish Family and Children's Service and relocated to Princeton, NJ, it now provides social work service, help with Jewish immigration, help for Holocaust survivors, individuals with disabilities, aids individuals sixty years and above, and people with disabilities who are experiencing age-related difficulties supervises. It also delivers Kosher Meals on Wheels and has a Kosher Café.

In addition, it enables seniors to enjoy a get-together; have a good meal; and good conversation once a month. The service also provides "Programs for Seniors," an Exercise Group with social activities.

See Appendix 3 – Philanthropic Organizations.

RELIGIOUS INSTITUTIONS

Har Sinai Hebrew Congregation - The great industrial complex of Trenton grew immediately before and after the Civil War. As a result, several houses of worship appeared. By 1850, several churches began in the City representing Presbyterian (remember Princeton College was a Presbyterian Seminary), Methodist (John Asbury had a mission in New Jersey), Baptist, Roman Catholic, Byzantine Catholic and other Christion denominations.

German Jews, in trickles, made their way to Trenton after the defeat of liberalism in the German States in 1848-9. This trickle formed a core Jewish community where none existed before. Accordingly, the Har Sinai Cemetery Association, formed on November 19, 1857 when eleven men met in the home of Morris Singer. Besides Mr. Singer, were Marcus Marx, Julius Schloss, Isaac Wymann, lgnatz Frankenstein, Lazarus Gottheim, Isaac Singer, Joseph Rice, Ephraim Kaufman, Marcus Aaron and Gustavus Cane.

A year later, its cemetery association committed to build a place of worship. Its initial religious services were held in private homes; then in rented quarters.

A September 1858 newspaper item tells us that 52 persons attended New Year's services in Temperance Hall, then located at the southeast corner of Broad and Front Streets. Formal services Har Sinai Hebrew Congregation building began in 1860.

Figure 16. Har Sinai Temple, 1902, Stockton Street

In 1860, its trustees were Simon Kahnweiler, Isaac Wymann, Henry Shoninger, Herman Rosenbaum, Marcus Aaron, Leon Kahnweiler and David Manko, most of them clothing merchants. Nearly all German, services and minutes were conducted in Hebrew and German. Kahnweiler, a prominent business figure, tried his hand at several ventures: manufacturing bricks, vinegar products, owning a grocery store and real estate.

Simon Kahnweiler became Har Sinai's first president, exercising considerable influence in the new congregation. Kahnweiler bought a Lutheran little brick chapel on the west side of North Montgomery Street, between Academy and Perry. It was refitted as a temple and dedicated with appropriate ceremonies on March 23, 1866.

Judge David Naar, an outstanding Jewish figure at that time, made the dedicatory address. Naar, was the former Mayor of Elizabethtown and Common Pleas Judge of Essex County, a member of the State Constitution of 1844, owner and publisher of the influential Daily True American, and a powerful figure in state Democratic councils. [31]

Rabbi Isaac Lesser, who with Rabbi Isaac Mayer Wise then shared the leadership of American Jewry, also spoke at the dedication. Lesser went on the found the Conservative movement in the 1880's. Wise established a Reform association in 1873 and a Rabbinical College in 1875.

There was some turmoil over Har Sinai's deed's provenance. The building was sold at Sheriff's auction in 1872. The deed was legally flawed was sold at a Sheriff's sale. There was a, heroine, however. Mrs. Toretta Kaufman, mother of Amelia Block and S.E. Kaufman, both pillars of the business community, saved the temple building.

Through her tireless efforts, she managed to collect sufficient funds so that by autumn of 1872, the congregation again owned the Montgomery Street property. Her daughter, Mrs. Amelia Kaufman Block, served actively for many years an active worker in the Har Sinai's Sisterhood.

The largest contributor was said to be Joseph Rice, a member, a leading merchant and one of Trenton's most respected citizens. He made up the balance needed after Mrs. Kaufman's proceeds.

As the German Jews in New York and Philadelphia, the Trenton's German Jews helped their obscurantist, callow Jewish breather when they arrived as immigrants. Not knowing anything of the language, customs, ways of doing business, etc., these German Jews instituted charitable societies to assist them in their new American environment.

Har Sinai sold its temple to Bayard Post, No.8, G.A.R. (Grand of the Republic) and in 1903, bought a lot at the southwest corner of Front and Stockton Streets to erect its second house of worship, dedicated on the evening of October 7, 1904. Soon after, the congregation engaged Rabbi Nathan Stern, a Reform rabbi. English replaced German in the services. Governor Woodrow Wilson gave a memorable address in the building in 1910.

In February 1922, the Board of Trustees joined the Union of American Hebrew Congregations (Reform movement). Shortly thereafter, the Temple found that increased school enrollment required a larger building. In 1925, Har Sinai purchased a lot on Bellevue Avenue, then a barren area, to erect Trenton's fourth house of Jewish worship. One of its members, Louis S. Kaplan served as architect. (He also designed the War Memorial Building.)

In 1929, Rabbi Abram Holtzberg became Har Sinai's spiritual leader. Others serving as officers were M. Lessler, Simon Rosenberg, Israel Goldvogel, Morris Ungerleider, Mr. Wagenheim, Mr. Schomberg, Mr.Kahn, Joseph Gabriel, L. Weiss, Mr. Bloch, Nathan Rosenau, Louis B. Michelson, Nathan Stern, Harry K. Jacobs, Joel Blau and Jacob Goldstein.

Figure 17. Har Sinai Temple 1929

The dedication ceremonies took place in September 1930. Important Rabbi's spoke at the dedication ceremony (Rabbi Louis Woolsey of Philadelphia, Dr. Julian Morgenstern, President of the Hebrew Union College, Rabbi Sidney Tedesche and Rabbi Alexander Lyons of Brooklyn). Julius Schafer was became Har Sinai's first President at its Bellevue Avenue location.[32] Although Har Sinai opened its new temple doors in the depression years of the 1930's, the congregation managed to carry on during difficult economic times. The temple was completely free of debt when it burned its mortgage on the evening of November 4, 1945. Rabbi Holtzberg's spiritual leadership continued for 25-years. Indeed, Dr. J.M. Schildkraut was president for many of twenty-five years, most of them overlapping Holzberg's.

To commemorate the initial Jewish presence in Trenton, the city government installed an official at 20 West State Street with the inscription:

Trenton's first Jewish organization, Mount Sinai Cemetery Association, formed November 19, 1857, later known as Har Sinai Hebrew Congregation, began regular synagogue services at this site in 1860.[33] —

With the death of Rabbi Holtzberg, Rabbi Joshua 0. Haberman, from a Buffalo congregation, replaced his colleague in 1951. Rabbi Haberman's rabbinate for the next eighteen years brought an extensive series of innovations, achievements and activities, which carried Har Sinai during the fifties and sixties through a period of unprecedented growth.

A significant addition to the worship services of Har Sinai took place in 1953 when Cantor Marshall M. Glatzer joined the Temple staff. In 1957, Har Sinai celebrated its Centennial chaired by Hon. Sidney Goldmann,

When Rabbi Haberman answered a call to serve as Rabbi for Washington Hebrew Congregation (one of the most prestigious Temples) in Washington, D.C. in 1969, Har Sinai called to its pulpit Rabbi Bernard Perelmuter from Erie, Pennsylvania, who served Har Sinai until June 1982.

In June 1982, Har Sinai welcomed Rabbi David J. Gelfand to its pulpit from Temple Beth El in Great Neck, New York. Then, came David Straus and Stuart A. Pollack. [34]

Congregation of the Brothers of Israel
('Acheinu B'nai Yisroel' – Orthodox, 1883)

Trenton's second oldest Jewish religious body (after the German Congregation, Har Sinai) is Congregation of the Brothers of Israel. This organization incorporated in 1883, but became functional four years later. Isaac Levy, a Scottish Jew (by way of Lithuania) became President for ten years in the 1890's.

Figure 18. Congregation Brother of Israel
(Acheinu B'nai Yisroel - now church)

Harry Podmore tells us that Brothers of Israel's first Trustees were Louis Levin, Louis Katz, Louis Lefkowitz, Abraham Bennestein, Abraham Goldstein, Jacob Hankelsky and Mr. Isaac Berman. Two years later, the synagogue purchased a cemetery on Vroom Street in Trenton.

In August 1887, the Trustees purchased the Union Street M.E. Church and converted it into a synagogue. On September 11, 1887, the remodeled edifice was dedicated. In 1900, the building was demolished and a new one was erected upon the site.

In 1885, the congregation established a place of burial on Vroom Street, adjoining Har Sinai Cemetery. In 1907, the place was enlarged by the purchase of an additional lot. In 1908, it served more than 1,200 families. And in 1913, an auxiliary cemetery was established near Cedar Lane, Hamilton Township. Its spiritual leader Rabbi Pinchus Turman, trained in Vilna.

The early officers of the Brothers of Israel congregation were: Hyman Silverman, president; Havis Olinsky, vice-president; Morris Iskovitz, secretary, and F. Lavinson, treasurer.

In 1908, the officers were Hyman Silverman, president; Havis; Jacob Fin, vice-president; Isaac Gutstein and Solomon Kohn, secretaries, and Zushman, treasurer.

Figure 19. Reserved Seat for tor Jewish Holidays, 1890's

In 1913, as the immigrants poured into South Trenton necessitated the congregation to purchase a larger cemetery on Cedar Lane.

Congregation People Of Truth (Anshei Emes – Orthodox,1891) - Congregation of the People of Truth (Anshei Emes) was an offshoot of the 1,200 family membership of Brothers of Israel. In 1902, the new congregation purchased the Second Presbyterian Church, on Union Street, refitted it for a synagogue; dedicated it on March 15, 1903.

In 1908, Rabbi Max Sufnoss was the spiritual leader of the People of Truth synagogue. He lived at 59 Union Street. Born in Vilna, Russia, he attended college in his native city; became a Rabbi. His first congregation was at Old Kinek, Province of Vilna. He immigrated to America in 1892. He was Rabbi of a New York congregation for about four years, and came to Trenton in 1896 at the call of the People of Truth congregation.

Figure 20. Anshe Emes (People of Truth)

Its officers were: President Peter Unger, Louis Kaplan, Isaac Goldman, Harry Kohn, Charles Smith, Harry Cooper. Isaac Goldman, Harry Kohn, Abraham Schultz and Solomon Jaffe. In 1893, the congregation established a cemetery near Cedar Lane, Hamilton Township.

Anshie Emes (People of Truth) congregation established two structures at Union and Fall streets: the synagogue and a school with a capacity of 200 students. Its two teachers were H. Hinkin and Hyman Vroblinsky. The Sabbath school's teachers were Miss Fannie Bushnon and Eleak Budsin.

Before he died, Isaac Levy (Levie), President of Brothers of Israel for ten years, was also President of this new congregation. His obituary is below:

ISAAC LEVY.

The First Russian to arrive in Trenton and who has
been Identified with every form of Activity
among his people. For a period of ten
years he was President of the
Brothers of Israel Con-
gregation.

Figure 21. Isaac Levy

Sketch of His Life

*The funeral service of Isaac Levy of 304 union street, one of
the oldest find *most prominent members - of the Jewish race in
South Trenton, who died Saturday, following a lingering illness of -
over a year) yesterday afternoon from his late residence at 4 o'clock;
Services- according to the Jewish rite by the Rev. Hersh Elitzer, of
the Synagogue of the Israelites Brotherhood.*

*Gathered around the coffin were the immediate members or the
family, while a lair number of relatives, friends and many who were
befriended in life, filled the house and the sidewalk in the vicinity.*

*Mr. Levy was one of the earliest Hebrews to settle in South
Trenton, where 'he has remained all his life, and from e first day his
chief mission was to aid - his countrymen. Being a contractor, the*

deceased was the promoter of the building of the present- beautiful synagogue of the Israelites' 'Brotherhood, of which he was a member, and the first and only free Hebrew school in Trenton.

He aimed unceasingly at Jewish progress, and to this end gave much time and money. His work with the members" of the congregation was met with their heartiest approval, and several medals were presented to him as a taken of their appreciation.

His labors did not cease even when the dread disease that removed him from life, first compelled him to retire from business. During the past nine months Mr. Levy organized and financed a project to help the poorer classes of his own people, a scheme which already, though its infancy, is doing great good among the Jews.

Mr. Levy was in his 70th year, and during his life has reared a family" of five children, who today show the fruits of their admirable training. They are Mary and Rachel, Abram, Bernard and Charles.

He was prominent in Jewish Masonic circles, and also was president of the People of Troth Society, a Jewish organization, whose members attended the funeral in a body.

Services at the grave consisted of eulogies delivered by a number of friends who knew him, honored him in life, and wished to pay fitting tribute to his memory before he was taken from their view. Interment was made in the Mount Sinai Cemetery, under the direction of Poulson and Coleman.

Interestingly, the Rabbi engaged at Anshei Emes shared his time with Congregation Brothers of Israel. The Shamas, who maintained the synagogues, was Dov Baer.

It should be noted that Isaac Levy began the first Talmud Torah, originally as an adjunct of Brothers of Israel congregation. Later on, it became fully independent.

In 1919, Rabbi Joseph Konowotz presided. In 1924, Rabbi Israel Bunin became Rabbi. [35]

Congregation Ahavath Israel (Hungarian Shul – Orthodox, 1909)

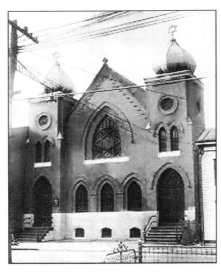

Figure 22. Congregation Ahavath Israel (Hungarian Shul)

Hungarian Jews were different from their Russian cousins. Hungarian Jews had lived in a different culture. Sandwiched between German, Russian and other Slovak Jews, cosmopolitan Hungarian Jews did not even speak Yiddish. Their customs were completely different. The Russian Jewish community considered them German. Non-cosmopolitan village Jews spoke Yiddish, sprinkled with Hungarian words (untranslatable to most Russian Jews).

The Hungarian language is unique (Finno-Ugrian language family). Further, although they were citizens of the Austro-Hungarian Empire, the government taught them to become invisible. Accordingly, the Magyars, with Jewish support, just tipped the balance of the population in Hungary.

Moreover, the Haskala movement (Western scientific, secular thinking) took hold in Hungary and Germany as opposed to most of obscurantist Russia/Poland. Hungary was a member of the Austro-Hungarian Empire.

Ethnically, Hungarian Jews were descended from those fleeing the Spanish expulsion. Afterwards, an enormous amount of Moravian and Bohemia (Czech) and Galician Jews arrived. They were citizens of the state as early as 1850. Consequently, although there was anti-Semitism, it was not on the same scale as other Eastern European countries.

When Hungarian Jews reached America, their natural inclination was to congregate together. Most Jewish Hungarians did not live in South Trenton. Rather, they lived in Chambersburg off Broad Street (between Dye St. and S. Clinton Ave).

Hungarian Jews initially belonged to the Russian synagogues (Brothers of Israel or Anshei Emes).

Some oral stories indicated that women began the movement for the new synagogue because they were not allowed proper ventilation in the balcony of the Anshe Emes on a hot Rosh HaShanah day in hot, humid Trenton.

During the next few months, members met in Rudner Hall on South Clinton Avenue. Meanwhile, Samuel Goldmann (Hon. Sidney Goldmann's father) rented his hall on South Broad St. to the new congregation. Shortly thereafter, the members rented Turner Hall on South Broad Street during the High Holy Days and Passover. A regular congregation (minyan) prayed in the home of its first religious leader, Rev. Max Gordon.

Because many congregants preferred to speak German or Hungarian rather than Yiddish, it became known as the "Hungarian shul," and in its early years, officials even accepted dues in Austrian currency.

Two months prior, twenty mostly Hungarian Jews met in the Trenton home of Henry Wirschafter, a prominent department store owner. On Dec. 23, 1909, the state chartered the Orthodox Congregation Ahavath Israel (Love of Israel).

Members remodeled the building (including placing two spires on the roof (in Hungarian style) and dedicated it to Jewish worship. The founders of the Congregation of Ahavath Israel were generally Austro-Hungarian. Its first officers and trustees were Samuel Goldmann, president, Leo Eisner, vice-president and Peter Littman, secretary. Trustees were Henry Wirtschafter, Herman Lefkowitz, Jacob Blaugrund, Louis Warady, Nathan Fuchs, Adolf L. Moskowitz and Armin Bonyai.

In 1911, the congregation purchased the Wesley Methodist Church on 439 Centre St. Its female members became very active in the activities of the Austrian-Hungarian Hebrew Ladies Society. In 1914, the shul organized a burial society and bought cemetery land in Hamilton Township in 1917. In the 1960's and 1970's, the congregation added two more cemetery sites.

In 1915, Ahavath Israel became the first Trenton's synagogue to join the Conservative movement and the first to hire an English-speaking rabbi to conduct services in English. Members collected funds for Jewish relief in World War I and received widespread praise for their endorsement of the Jewish Community Center in 1916. Interestingly, Hungarian Jews founded the American Cigar Company originally owned by a Hungarian Jew named S. Seidenberg who sold it the American Tobacco Company (on Division St) at the turn of the 20th century. Employing over 1,000 workers, including immigrant Cubans, its management consisted of Hungarian Jews: Albert Gold, the families Kasser, Greenwald, Lazlo, Loeb and Louis Gross. Later on, another factory was added on College and Division Streets. During the Great Depression, when most of the industrial giants ceased to produce, the American Cigar Company kept on working. In the 1950's, automatic cigar machines eventually replaced the individually wrapped cigars made in Trenton. Two other cigar companies also operated at a lessor scale: Cigar FaCo (Sam Levy); Mopo Cuba (Isador Klein).[36]

The other factory that kept busy during the depression was the Horsman Doll Factory, also owned by a Hungarian Jew, Harry Freidman.

Its, membership shrank as members moved westward. It continued to offer holiday programming and adult education classes, but became economically unfeasible to sustain.

In 2009, the synagogue merged with Congregation Adath Israel. Names on a memorial plaque: Applebaum, Alter, Bogart, Cohen, Durvitz, Durshstrom, Fier, Gelston, Gilman, Gold, Goldman, Goldstein, Greenwald, Gross, Herkovitz, Hersh, Introlligator, Kahn, Kasser, Knoff, Lefkowitz, Levy, Markowitz Masmir, Reich, Saaz, Small, Stern, Tankel, Vatitz, Vellowstein and Wertshafter.

Figure 23. American Cigar Company, Grand Ave

42

Figure 24. American Cigar Company, Spanish Motif, Grand Ave

On April 12, 2010, the New Jersey Jewish News ran a story about the closing of Ahavath Israel, saying "Now that the merger between Ahavath Israel Congregation and Adath Israel Congregation has been overwhelmingly approved, all that remains is the paperwork", said Rabbi Daniel Grossman of Adath Israel. The congregation merged with Adath Israel in October 2010.[37]

People of Righteousness (Anshei Tzedek, 1907)

A social organization, which sometimes doubled as a small congregation, called 'Anschie Chedek' (People of Justice), founded in October 1907. Meyer Rabinowitz, a sanitary expert became its spiritual leader.

This congregation held its functions the second floor St. of 6 Union Street. The congregation reported over 100 members. Soon disbanded as a synagogue, the membership decided to become a social organization, only.[38]

Congregation Workers of Truth (Orthodox- Anshei Fife, 1919)

Congregation of the Workers of Truth filed incorporation papers in 1919. The Anshe Fife, 'the small shul,' sat a few doors down from Anshei Emes. A few years later the organization purchased two dwellings on Union Street, near Market Street, and remodeled them into a house of worship.

Figure 25. Anshe Fife (Workers of Truth)

The first officers of the People of Truth congregation were: S. Silverman, president; Jacob Fein, vice-president; Isaac Gutstein and Solomon Kohn, secretaries, and Zushman Fein, treasurer. The trustees of this congregation were Jacob Albert and Mr. Saperstein.

Although there is little evidence of this small shul, Rabbi Eliezer Mayer Preil (later to move to Elizabeth), Rabbi Kantorowitz and his son-in-law, Rabbi Mordchai Lev provided rabbinic leadership. Its 1955, officers were President, Morris Forman; vice president; Jess Fagelman; treasurer; David Binder; and trustees Joseph Reil, Morris Rubin and Sam Cohen.

Congregation Adath Israel (Conservative, 1923)

Traditional Russian Jews started a New York City seminary in 1888. Rabbi Sabato Morais led the institution but it closed after his death in 1897. Nevertheless, with the help of German Jews, such as Jacob Schiff, Louis Marshall, the Lewisohns, the Guggenheims and a number of other established Jews, a new Conservative movement raised $500,000 to build another Jewish Theological Seminary in New York in 1903. Dr. Solomon Schechter, an Oxford professor, served as its first Chancellor. From this institution came all Rabbis of Adath Israel in Trenton .

In Alexander Budson's legal office, a committee formed to build another synagogue in the Western section of Trenton. Committee members were: Alexander Budson, David Gross, Solomon Urken Harry Millner, Harry Bernstein, Harry I. Gross, Samuel Lavinthal, Joseph Lavine, I. S. Rednor, Samuel Levin, Michael Galinsky, Israel Kohn, Harry Siegle, Israel Goldberg, and Israel Vine.

At the opening, the Toast Master was Alexander Budson. Speakers were Rabbi Holzberg (Har Sinai), Mayor Donnelly, Rabbi Israel Bunin (Brother of Israel and Anshei Emes), and the Rector of St. Michaels's Methodist Episcopal Church.[41]

This synagogue served a large role in providing education, social and spiritual facilitates for those Trentonians who moved from South Trenton to West Trenton. Together with Har Sinai Temple, they hosted most of Jewish synagogue membership from the 1950's onward.

The synagogue moved to Lawrenceville in 1987 from its Trenton moorings. Ahavath Israel, another Conservative synagogue merged with it.

Zionism

Zionists believed that Israel should be the national Jewish homeland. At the time, the territory, called Palestine by the Romans, belonged to the Ottoman Empire. After World War I, it became a British protectorate.

Zionism triggered dual nationalistic feelings for Israel and the country of current residence. Interestingly, Zionism was never a big issue in old Trenton. Trenton Jews felt secure in the 'new' country.' Indeed, Rabbi Lavinthal and of Philadelphia and Rabbi J. I. Bluestone of New York returned from the first Zionist Congress in Basle, Switzerland (1898) to spread the message. In that year, Trenton's Jews formed Sons of Zion (B'nai Tzion) with Isaac J. Millner as President and David Aroniss as secretary. Meetings were held at both Brothers of Israel and People of Truth Synagogues. Incorporators were A. M. Elfman, Isaac A. Onkelsky, Samuel Brodner, Frank Morris and Nathan Aroniss.

In 1905, the local body affiliated with the national organization, the Federation of American Zionists. Officers were Albert H. Millner (President); Robert Lavine, Vice-President); M. Cohn, (Secretary) and B., Budson, (Treasurer).

Again, in 1911, they affiliated with a reconstituted national organization, Order of Sons of Zion, a fraternal and benevolent society. Its leaders were Hyman Forer, Dr. Fuchs, Harry Heller, Reuben Lavine, Albert Millner, Max Movshovitz, Henry Millner, Rev. Max Gordon, Mendel Dietz, Joseph Radinsky and David L. Samachson.

However, there was a disagreement as to what type of Zionism it should be. One branch (Mizrachi) thought the Jewish state should be a religious state. The Paoli Zionists felt Israel should be a socialist, secular nation. Hyman Levi, David Lavine and Rabbi Kantorowitz led the Mizrachi movement. Samson Donskoy, 56 Union St, led the Paoli Zionist branch. He and Nathan Kramer were its leaders, operating from Warren St., below Falls St. in South Trenton.

The Zionist organizations, through the World Jewish Congress, funded the Zionist movement with its resettlement and educational activities.

The Ladies' Zion Aid Society incorporated in 1900. Trustees were Rebecca Lavinson, Hende Bash, Elke Galinsky, Dora Goodstein and Charles Bash. Headquarters were on 100 Union St.

Jewish Day School

Trenton had its own full-time religious educational institution, a Talmud Torah. A Talmud Torah was an all Day School where youth learn Hebrew, Jewish traditions and religious precepts of Orthodox Judaism. Dr. Herzl's Zion Hebrew School on Union Street began as an adjunct of Congregation of the Brothers of Israel in 1894. Prior to this time, there was an improvised Hebrew school held in a rented hall on Union Street near Fall Street.

In 1904, the Trustees erected a Hebrew school house (the first of its kind in Trenton) on Union Street, opposite the Brothers of Israel and named it in memory of Dr. Theodor Herzl, father of political Zionism, who died during the same month that the cornerstone was laid (July 1904). The building was subsequently sold to the city for a public school house. This school resumed operations in the 1910's on Cooper and Market Str.

In 1926, its officers were: Harry Haveson, President; Max Lit, Vice-President; Abe Harris, Treasurer, Rabbi Isaac Bunin, Supervisor; Rev. Morris Boros, Principal and Mark Mishkin, Teacher.

MAJOR PHILANTHROPIC AND
SOCIAL INSTITUTIONS

The Progress Club - Rich Jews created The Progress Club. Most of its members were prosperous Jewish businessmen and professionals. Starting in November 1894 as the Young Men's Hebrew Club, with a membership of twenty-seven, held its first meetings on South Broad Street, below Factory Street. The Club later moved to East State Street, between Broad and Warren Streets. Arthur Schwartz was the first president of the old club, which was interested in improving the mental, moral, social and physical conditions of its members to protect Jewish interests. [38]

About 1905, the club changed into a purely social one, and adopted the name of the Progress Club. New quarters were acquired in the Alhambra Building in downtown Trenton. Subsequently, the Thropp property on 534 East State Street became the club's headquarters.

In 1922, the members bought from John S. Broughton estate at 178 West State Street, now the newer N.J.E.A. building. [39]

Dr. Samuel Freeman was the first president after the establishment of the Progress Club; Barnett Elting was vice-president; A. Siegel, treasurer; and Philip Papier, secretary.

In 1925, the Progress Club men bought a country place on the Lawrenceville Road, where they have established a golf club. After this purchase, the official name changed to the Progress City and Country Club.

Consisting of mostly successful German Jewish businessmen who also attended Har Sinai Temple, they used the club to host Temple functions.

Its officers in 1901: M. A. Fuld, President; S. Kahn, Vice President; Sol Papier, Secretary. The Governing Board: S. Kahn; P. Lazarus; A. Klinkowstein; M.A. Fuld; L. A. Fuld; L. L. Friedman; A. Seigel; E. R. Fox; S. Levy; Sol Papier; and William Vogel.[41]

In 1913, the *Evening Times* reported that the Progress Club held a ladies' night last evening in the form of a banquet in its rooms in the Mechanics Building. After the feast five hundred were played. Those who were awarded favors were Mrs. Isaac Goldberg. Mrs. Samuel Freeman, Miss Fannie Grumbacher of York,

Pa., Theodore Tobish, Philip Goldman and Julius Schafer. The committee comprised William Vogel, Samuel Levy and Philip Lazarus. [42]

In 1914, Mrs. Jonas A. Fuld hosted a Card party at the club, to raise $1,500 for transportation costs for 200 summer camp children. [43]

In 1914, the Progress Club located to 534 East State Street; the club rented quarters from the majestic estate located at 534 East State St to 1919. Thereafter, it moved to 22 ½ North Warren Street on the second and third floors. In 1922, it located to the Broughton Home on 178 West State Street. Its next move was to Lawrenceville Road in June 1926. This location housed a club and a golf course. [45]

One of these Jewish golfers became champion of the county; however, Chick Bash was denied entry into a local private country club. To accommodate Jewish golfers, Greenacres Country Club incorporated as a nonsectarian club. Nothing in the certificate of incorporation indicates that it was an exclusively Jewish club. The charitable requirement of Greenacres, in fact, indicated that Jewish members were required to give annual donations to the Trenton Jewish Federation; non-Jewish members could give their charitable contribution to the United Way (Larger community charity).

Figure 26. Greenacres Country Club Entrance

Harry Friedman, the owner of the Horseman Doll Factory, with the assistance of three banks (Trenton Trust, Broad Street Bank and First Mechanics) largely provided financing for the Greenacres Club (originally secured from the bankruptcy court). The Trenton Trust Banking Company managed the mortgage.

In order to protect the equity in the land from any losses in the operations of the country club, the members formed the Greenacres County Club Holding Company and transferred all lands to this holding company. Subsequently, led by Leon Levy, Esq., its early members donated cash to the holding company in exchange for shares.

Greenacres Country Club has been a social and recreational haven for members residing in Mercer County, NJ, Bucks County, PA and the Princeton area for three quarters of a century. The Club now encompasses over 150-acres and includes a pristine 18-hole golf course and a full service golf professional shop. There is also a complete tennis facility with eight courts and pro shop sit near the pool facilities with pool house and snack bar close by. The culture of the Club is an active, family group, giving to charitable organizations.[46]

Figure 27. 'Y" Basketball Team 1925

Jewish Community Center (YMHA-YWHA) – American Judaism lived outside of the synagogue. Deborah Dash Moore, for example, shows that B'nai B'rith functioned as a "secular synagogue," seeking a refuge for those emancipated Jews dissatisfied with mainstream Judaism. Tony Fels made a related argument in his detailed study of "Jews and Freemasonry in Gilded-Age San Francisco. Similar arguments could be made about the rise of Ethical Culture as well as about the whole Jewish Social Justice movement — a more secular approach to make life more meaningful in America.[47]

For Russian and German Jews, American Judaism also existed outside of the synagogue. Deborah Dash Moore, for example, shows that B'nai B'rith functioned as a "secular synagogue," seeking a refuge for those emancipated Jews dissatisfied with mainstream Judaism.[48] Similar arguments were made about the rise of the Ethical Culture Society and the whole Jewish Social Justice movement — a more secular approach to make Jewish life more meaningful in America.

Trenton had its own Young Man's Hebrew Club, one of the first social organizations appearing in documents.

Frencis Bazley Lee, in her History of Trenton published the *Trenton State Gazette* in 1895, provides the earliest evidence of a Jewish social grouping with names. The Young Man's Hebrew Club operated from 26 East State Street. Its officers were: Samuel Kahn; Vice-President, Ephraim Fuld; Treasurer, Abe Siegel; Secretary, James Bernard; Financial Secretary, F. Mandell, Sergeant-at-Arms, Dan Black.

The entertainment committee consisted of P. Lazarus, M. Grumbacher, and J. Cohn. The library committee: M. Fuld; C Cohn and J. Bernard. The membership committee: D. Block and H. Frank.

A permanent institution, the Young Men's Hebrew Association began on December 5, 1909 at the home of William Haveson on South Broad Street. Officers of the new association were Joseph Stone, president; David Josephson, vice-president; Charles Gilinsky, secretary; and Joseph Bulitsky, treasurer. Board of governors were William Haveson, Herman Haveson, and Barney Lavine.

Charter members were: Charles Gilinsky, Harry Levinson, Joseph Stone, David Josephson, M. Appelstein, William Haveson, Barney Lavine, Joseph Bulitsky, L. Fromkin, Herman Haveson, Samuel Swernofsky and Isaac Bulitsky. The fee for charter members was $1.00 and dues, fifteen cents a week.

At the sixth meeting, the committee paid a deposit on rooms owned by Dr. William Julian on South Broad Street. The Y.M.H.A.-Y.W.H.A. was the first Jewish "Y" to establish a home and have a paid executive secretary.

Its officers in 1917 were: David Holzner, president; Samuel Levy, first vice-president; Jonas Fuld, second vice-president; Harry Haveson, third vice-president; Isaac Goldberg, secretary; Dr. Harry K. Jacobs, secretary, and Charles Fishberg.

The first Director was David L. Feldman; followed by Sidney Marcus, who was succeeded by Maurice Bisgyer. Dr. M. H. Chaseman, Mr. Bisgyer and Haym Peretz (1929).[49]

In 1921, the membership finding that its quarters were too small, acquired the front part of the building. The first baseball game recorded the "Y" playing the Adelphi Club. Players were Lavinson, catcher, Sutnick, pitcher; Applestein, first base; Lavine, second base; Freeman, shortstop; J. Bulitsky, third base; Budson, left field; Haveson, center field; and Glazier, substitute. The club also fielded a basketball team.

In 1915, Rabbi Samuel Thurman, Har Sinai, discussed the desirability of merging several organizations into the new "Y." In 1916, the Audax Club (Herman Malkowitz), the Adelphi Club (Philip. Vine), the Young Judea Club (Mr. Jaffey) merged with the "Y."

Basketball: Melding German and Russian Jews

American Jews became sportsman. Although they fielded a baseball team, their passion was basketball. Jewish basketball players served as an expression of Jewish ethnic identity, an important part of modern American Jewish culture as well as contributing to the game.

Figure 28. Mike Bloom

The Community Centers (Y.M.H.A.'s) encouraged youngsters by organizing basketball leagues. The Community Center experience broke social barriers between the German and Russian Jews. Jews experienced difficulty competing outside the Jewish community. In 1946, CCNY Coach Nat Holman's documented that an offending college coach actually used extremely derogatory anti-Semitic terms, when playing in New York.[50]

Meyer (Mike) Bloom was Trenton basketball's greatest product. At 6 ft., 6 inches Bloom towered over everyone. Learning his skills at the YMHA, he put his height and skill for the community center and later to high school, college and professional teams.

In the 1930's, the basketball rules gave a gargantuan advantage to tall players and/or high jumpers because of 'jump balls.' Until 1936, after every score, there was a 'jump ball'. Moreover, until 1981, 'jump balls' resolved 'tied' possessions.

Newspaper accounts in the Trenton Evening Times told the story of Bloom's controlling almost all 'tip-offs.'[51] e led Trenton Central High School to three state championships (1932-1934). He next starred as an All-American at Temple University.

Figure 29. Trenton High School 1935 State Champs, towering Mike Bloom on far left

After college, Mike played professional basketball until 1950 (Before the National Basketball Association), with the Trenton Tigers, the Baltimore Bullets and the Boston Celtics.[52]

Ed Alpern wrote a paean to Benny Olinsky and deservedly so. Benny Olinsky and Harry Olinsky were two of Trenton's basketball prodigies, developed by the "YMHA." Both played for the vaunted State Champion Trenton High teams in the mid-1930.

In the early 1950's, Ben Olinsky coached. He also started the Biddy League. One of the Biddy League's participants was a youngster named Tal Brody, who became an All-State basketball guard in Trenton High's wining 1964 season. An All-American at Illinois, he was the 12th draft choice in the NBA draft and an Israeli Olympian in 1972.[53]

In 1977, became Israel's 'Mr. Basketball. "He led Israel's basketball team to the European Cup Basketball Championship, by besting an almost professional Red Army team (CSKA Moscow). Brody remarked: "We are on the map! And we are staying on the map – not only in sports, but in everything," a phrase repeated used for decades from political speeches to National Lottery commercials.

Figure 30. Tal Brody lighting torch for Maccabiad Games, Israel

Brody stayed in Israel. He married an Israeli and raised children there. His basketball award include the Israel Prize, University of Illinois "Man of the Year," an inductee into the International Jewish Sports Hall of Fame inducted the U.S. National Jewish Sports Hall of Fame. [54]

In 1955, reflective of the Jewish population shift, the 'Y' moved to Lower Ferry Road in nearby Ewing Township. World famous architect, Louis Kahn, designed the bathhouses, now listed in the National Register of Historic Places in 1984.

Figure 31. National Register Louis Kahn's Bathhouse at JCC

Other Charitable and Social Organizations

The Bikur Cholim Society cared for the sick. There also were similar societies in Trenton: The Hebrew Charity Society, New American Club, The Hebrew Charitable Association, and the South Trenton Ladies' Bikur Cholim Society.

In August 1893, the Hebrew Charity Society organized with 35 members. Supported from monthly dues, contributions and money raised by a social event, its first officers were: President, Manus E. Fuld; vice-president, Louis A. Cohen; secretary, Adolph Adler; and treasurer, Rev. Israel Gabriel. This society had originally been the Har Sinai Charity Society.

In 1902, the Hebrew Charity Society grew to 59 persons. The officers at that time: President, Nathan Rosenau; Vice-president, Louis Cohen; Secretary, Jonas A. Fuld; and Treasurer, Louis A. Fuld.

It assisted destitute travelers by establishing a sheltering home on Union Street. Its charity balls given in the old Masonic Temple, northwest corner of Warren and State Streets, were renowned.

In February 1908, Hebrew Charity Society moved to a new headquarters at 612 So. Warren St, Trustees were John Frankel, Jacob Fine, and Samuel Stone.

The South Trenton Ladies' Bikur Cholim Society formed by Mr. and Mrs. J. Levine Mrs. H. Levy, Mr. and Mrs. E. Watov, Mr. and Mrs. Lenzner, Mr. and Mrs. Zimskind, Mr. And Mrs. Sachs, Mrs. Albert, Mrs. Ziegler, and Mrs. Meltzer. Officers were: President – Mrs. Escovitz; Treasurer, Mrs. Simanisky; Secretary,

Mrs. Simanisky. Its trustees were Jennie Lefkowitz, Minnie Barboriski, Gussie Simanisky, Rose Habas, Fannie Marshall, Lebbey Heller and Hyman Siminisky.

For a society devoted entirely to Americanization work was the New American Club. In 1921, Miss-Mamie Levin was largely instrumental in its founding and was supported by Sydney Marcus, secretary of the Y. M. H. A. Its activities included a familiarization of the English language, political and economic elements of the US, literary programs, both in English and Yiddish.

In 1905, Workingman's Circle, Branch 90, established a Mutual Benefit Society in Trenton The Workmen's Circle or Arbeter Ring (אַרבעטער-רינג) was a Yiddish language American Jewish fraternal organization committed to social justice and Jewish culture. The national organization once provided old age homes, schools, summer camps, meeting hall, health insurance and cultural events, most in the Yiddish language.

In 1905, another group formed Branch 222. Its first meeting, organized by Joseph Spector, Mr. Gunbrow and several other intellectuals, met at 57 Union Street. In additional to fraternal benefits, the Society offered a program of literary discussions and debates on current topics. The Hebrew Debating and Mutual Aid Society also merged with Workman's Circle.

Hebrew Immigration Mutual Aid Society

Ed Grad continued his community services by establishing "HIMAS" (Hebrew Immigration Mutual Aid Society) to assist the adjustment of immigrant Jews. HIMAS, along with the Free Loan society transacted modest loans to immigrants starting their businesses. This group also offered mutual benefits (life insurance, burials).[55]

This national organization, pro-Zionist, known for its help for the working class and socialist tendencies, held a membership of more than 1,000 at its height. Its activities included began a workers loan fund, an immigrant aid society and helped other Jewish communities after World War 1. Later, it devoted itself to homeless Jews and the elderly finally resulting in an old age home. It also backed concerts, debates, lectures, dramas and classes to learn English. Ed Grad was the dynamo behind the success of this organization.

Its leaders were Edwin Grad, Joe Yuris, Abe Factor, Nathan and Esther Spector, Jake Hafitz, Fannye Spector Corosh, Nathan Goldstein, Sarah Adelman.

In 1915, both these branches merged as Branch 222. Its officers were: President Ed Grad and Trustees, Solomon Sharlin, Robert Thome, Joseph Spector, Paul Urken and Abe Factor.

In 1917, they established the first American Yiddish School, which taught 60 students, staffed New York experts, the school stopped in 1918 as a result of the Influenza Epidemic. Nevertheless, in 1923, the school resumed, moving to 157-9 Mercer St., which later became the Labor Lyceum.

In the 1920's, active members included Michael Charnovsky, Reubin Orlin, Morris Nabutovsky, Elsie Schwartz, Louis Williams, Clara Horowitz, Eva Rubin, Tillie Horowitz and Samson Donsey.

The first Yiddish School and Workman's Circle School in Trenton, opened at 33 Market Street, previously a movie theater and later Herman Spiegel's furniture store. Later a Ladies Auxiliary joined this group. The group was very active and joined forces with the USO during World War II.

Drama and Theater

Harry Gerofsky mentioned that South Trenton was like a mini-shtetl. He goes on to talk about theatre groups in Trenton. Local players featured plays at the Spector Theatre at 105 Lamberton St. Professional players featured plays at the Grand Theatre on South Broad Street.[56]

Ed Grad, whom you met at the Workingmen's Circle, also activated "The Little Theater Group," presenting Yiddish plays and other cultural activities in the 1910's. Some of its 'artsy' participants were Joe Yarus, Abe Factor, Nathan and Esther Spector, Jake Horowitz, Fanny Spector Corosh, Nathan Goldstein, Sarah Adelman.

Another theater group, known as The New Era Literary Society attracted intellectuals, want-to-be thespians and the out-of-town Jewish students attending the Normal School (now The College of New Jersey).Their first meetings were held in Star Hall, South Broad Street, and later in the Arcade Building. Rehearsals were on Sundays. The organization materially contributed to the cultural milieu with its discussions of books and plays, mock trials, debates, one of their literary products was a monthly paper, The New Era Journal, edited by Fannie Dushman.

The first annual banquet of the New Era Literary Society was held Sunday November 29, 1908. The officers were: John S. Rubin, President; Jennie Cohn, vice-president; Bessie Rosenberg, treasurer; Anna Gerson, secretary. Later, Miss

Fannie Fannie Dushman became president. (She ultimately married Alexander Budson.) Others members were Louis Lavinson, Lou Litt; Kate Gerson, Bella Bloom, Joe Kohn, Dr. William Julian, Simon Lenzner and Morris Millner.

Later the organization changed its name to the Audax Club. Later officers were: Lewis Gerofsky, president; Louis Schragger, vice-president; "Nat" Elitzer, secretary; end Irving Lasky, treasurer. The second annual vaudeville and dance in 1915 showcased an overture by Laskey's orchestra, (Crescendo Four), Harry Montgomery, humorologist; Pauline Carr, singing comedienne; Three Lyceum Boys, comedians; "Nat" Elitzer, vocalist; and an original comedy sketch written and produced by Harry Mendelsohn and Samuel Hammerman entitled, "Painful Partners." Other cast members were Sam Pincus, Samuel Hammerman; Hyman Goldfarb, Harry Mendelsohn; Miss Carey (stenographer), Miss Violet Flowers, Harry N. Weiss and Joseph M. Whalen.

Those names identified with The Audax Club were Hyman Meltzer, Max Magaliff, Louis Hammerman, Samuel J. Luria, Samuel Goldston, Robert Gilman, S. S. Richmond, "Nat" Elitzer, Harry Mendelsohn, Isidor H. Meltzer, Phil E. Lavine, Elliot Stern, Samuel Snyderman, Max Rosenthal, Joseph Teitz, Louis Zlochn, Joseph Pell, Jack Rosenthal, Herman R. Mallowitz, Harry N. Weiss, David Warach, Morris Urken, Samuel Berkowitz, Albert Rothstein, Jacob Rednor, Benjamin Elitzer, Irving Lasky, Morris Caster, Samuel Gladstone, Louis Schragger, Morris Lipman, Samuel Portin, M. Applestein, Lewis Gerofsky and others. The Audax Club ultimately merged with the Y. M. H. A.[57]

Jacob Gordon Hebrew Dramatic Club

Benches collapsing, actors falling off the stage were only some of the antics presented at Jacob Gordon Hebrew Dramatic Club. To put on a production was a 'production.' The actors rehearsed for months. The producers made elaborate scenic and costume designs.

Nathan Spector creating Trenton's Yiddish theater, copying New York. He converted 105 Lamberton Street into a small theater. Fitted with side boxes and stage equipment, including footlights and some sceneries, the seating capacity was 150. Admission was five cents. Actors used the basement as changing rooms. Shows were on Friday nights. Among those identified with this amateur theater were Bessie Shein, Sarah Adelman, Joseph Spector, Sr., Joseph Spector, Jr., David Gordon, Max Sufness, Samuel Popkin, Harry Harrison, Nathan Goldstein,

Jacob Wulkin, Jacob Radnor, Sarah Redden, Mat Hilda Spector, Dora Berman and Mrs. Applstein. [58]

Later the Papier family established the Star Theater in downtown Trenton. Solomon and Philip Papier, originally operated a theater in his native Amsterdam, Holland. Solomon Papier arrived in Trenton when he was 19 years old. Enterprisingly, he became a clothier operating three stores. The third clothing business was atop the Star Theater.

The Star became Trenton's first "Nickelodeon., an American phenomenon that showed early cinema to the curious public for recreation. Nickelodeons typically seated fewer than 200 with a film screen hung on the back wall, a piano (and maybe a drum set) in addition to the movie projector.

Russian-Turkish Baths

Brought from Russia, there were two bathhouses (shvitz) on Union St. in the early 1900's.

The Audix Club was an early secular social club that ultimately merged with the"Y." Charter members were Charles Galinsky, Harry Levinson, Joseph Stone, David Josephson, M. Applstein, William Haveson, Barney Lavine, Joseph Bulitsky, L. Fromkin, Herman Haveson, Samuel Swernofsky and Isaac Bulitsky.

The Kachunkie

Len Silverstein reports that the Liberty Club based at the end of Union Street, near, what is now Highway Route 29, was a club of young men who played cards. Also called the 'Kachunkie' this club was renowned for its competitive and high stakes games.

The 'Kachkunie' was a men's gambling club. Known for its high-stakes and risk-takers, it also performed charity work among South Trenton's needy children.

Chartered by the state of New Jersey, its members were primarily Jewish men from South Trenton (there were also a few Italians). Its formal name was the South Trenton Liberty Association. At its height, the Kachunckie numbered over 100 members. [59]

Other Clubs

Other Trenton Jewish clubs were The Progressive Republican Club (1908), Capitol City Lodge, No. 51, Free Sons of Israel, Independent Order of Ahavas Achim (1893), Independent Order of the Sons of Jacob, Capitol City Lodge, No. 64 (1908), The Farus Club (1916), Jewish Socialist-Territorialist Labor Party of America, B'Nai Brith, Young Women's Hebrew Association, The Sphinx Club, The New American Club, The Deborah Society.

Trenton's Young Judaea Association formed in February 1913. Its president for many years was Simon Rednor. The club headquarted at 10 Union St.

Harry Podmore recounts a True Gazette Story in 1913 revealing that Lewis Selesnick was the general chairman of committees; Harry Rednor, in charge of sports." [60]

Cemeteries

Har Sinai Cemetery Association formed Trenton's first Jewish cemetery on November 19, 1857. In the same year, it purchased a lot at the corner of Vroom and Liberty Streets. Its founders were: Marcus Marx, Julius Schloss, Isaac Wymann, Morris Sanger, lgnatz Frankenstein, Lantos Golheim, Isaac Sanger, Joseph Rice, Ephraim Kaufman, Marcus Aron and Gustavus Cane.[61]

See Appendix 2.

Mikveh (Jewish Ritual Bath)

A Mikveh (Jewish Ritual Bath) seems out of place in modern society. A carry-over from Temple times when bodily purification led to spiritual purification, each shtetl possessed a ritual bath. And Trenton's Jews transplanted the ritual purity idea to Trenton.

Jewish law specifies that a Mikveh must draw its water from an external source (rain, oceans, rivers, wells, and spring-fed lakes), although piping could supplement the baths.

Originally, both sexes used the Ritual baths. Over time, women after their menses used the mikveh. The Mikveh also used to purify items that became impure (kosher silverware, china, etc.) and for conversions.

Initially, its location was the basement of the Brothers of Israel Hebrew School; then it found its own home on Fall St. Thereafter, a permanent structure remained until urban renewal demolition in the 1950's on 'V' where Union and Decatur Streets met.

Trenton Jewish Federation

As mentioned before, Jews practiced philanthropy at the local level. Eventually, organizations found that their fund-raising and social events conflicted with other. To resolve this issue as the population grew, Boston formed a federation of agencies in 1895.

Federations grew in numerous cities and towns. In Trenton, a Jewish Federation appeared in 1929, acting as a clearinghouse for philanthropic efforts, the Federations undertook planning for the Jewish communities.

The Jewish Federation also performed planning for the future needs of the local community and may assist agencies in other ways. Its first leaders were Louis B. Rudner, Carl B. Shipper and Rose Galinsky.

Abrams Foundation

The Home for the Aged Sons and Daughters of Israel (Greenwood House) organized in 1939. Currently it provides 132 beds for intensive care. In addition, The Abrams Foundation donated an assisted living facility. The Abrams family consist of two brothers, Samuel and David, and sister, Susan. The Abrams Foundation also helped finance the activities of the Abrams Day Camp, a Jewish day camp and other children's activities.

Trenton's Jews were well-integrated in the communal life of the city, participating actively in the United Fund and other charitable and educational institutions.

SOCIO-ECONOMIC CONTRIBUTION

Trenton Jewish Community in Transition: *Assimilation, 1920-1960*

During the period of 1920 to 1968, one school of thought posited that U.S., Jewish America assimilated and subsequently amalgamated in the American culture. An alternative view stated that Judaism continued in America, evolving into its new environment. The late theologian, Mordechai Kaplan, maintained that Judaism was an evolving civilization.

Gottlieb designs criteria of Judaism: food (kosher/non-kosher); nostalgic reference to the European experience; US patriotism; American sport/leisure as detracting/attracting in terms of Jewish identity; Jewish entertainment (culture, music, theater); secular entertainment (culture, music, theater); Jewish education; frequency of religious practice; secular education; Jewish political mobilization (i.e. Israel support, Jewish organization memberships); secular political mobilization (i.e. political party, environment etc.)[62] Jon Hess indicated that assimilation makes an insider from an outsider. Depending on where you are located in the assimilationist scale, the insider feels part of the group, shares its values and easily fits in. At the other end of this scale, accommodation is part of the adaptation process. The process of accommodation involves altering one's values because of new (foreign) stimuli.[63] Hence, there were numerous interpretations of Jewish identity.

This assimilation/accommodation period presents the immigrant seeking opportunities of an education; competing in sports; achieving professional success and earning respect as businessmen. They felt caught in the middle of their parents ('Old Country') and 'normal' society.

Typical of this phase is, during 1920-1960, the Jewish "Y" movement integrated disparate Jewish communities (German, Russian, Polish, Romanian, and Hungarian, and Galician).

The Jewish community also defended itself from anti-Semitism from the "old Stock' Americans, which formed a xenophobic group to cease immigration from Southern Eastern Europe; and from the Ku Klux Klan, so prevalent in the United States through the early 1920's. The Klan, not known for its subtlety, intimidated minorities, Blacks and recent immigrants. 'Leaders" of society established quotas for admission to higher education and admission into the professions and corporate worlds. Political anti-Semitism evidenced itself by political parties ignoring the pleas to avoid victimization.

During this period, Jewish hospitals arose to welcomed Jewish physicians denied privileges in other hospitals. Because Jews were not accepted in the large law and accounting firms, major Jewish accounting and law firms formed. And the German Jewish financial business partnered with Russian Jews.

'Gloomy' is the word best describing Trenton's 1934-36 period. Following the stock market crash in late 1929, the nation's worst economic depression severely taxed the resources of the Trenton Jewish community. Mikveh use abated as Trenton's Jews adapted to the general community. Trenton's Mikveh ceased when Urban Renewal condemned the area to build state buildings, although there are two small ones in local synagogues.

According to the Consumer Expenditure Survey for 1934–36, a family's annual savings stood at $11.[64]

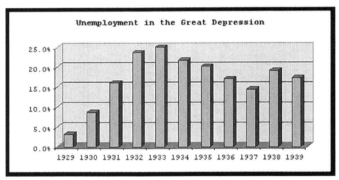

Figure 32. Unemployment in Great Depression

Amalgamation Period, 1960-1980

Amalgamation is the last stage of assimilation. Heterogamy (marrying out of the faith), means that Jews began to marry non-Jews. Positive attributes include many of the characteristics of the second movement. Going one-step further, the Jewish American was comfortable living in his suburban community in a mixed neighborhood, often segregated by socio-economic groupings.

Comparison to Other Communities

Trenton's Jewish community was not unique in establishing a town within a town when its Russian immigrants arrived. Springfield/Belmont, a onetime prominent Jewish immigration neighborhood located in Newark, New Jersey, as well as Schenectady also had the characteristics of a shtetl. Researching the communities of Schenectady, Newark, St. Paul and part of Philadelphia, Trenton's Jewish experience followed along practically similar lines, except the needles trades were not a large factor in the Trenton Jewish economy. [65]

The largest initial businesses were the junk business and the liquor business, which was a carryover from Poland and part of Russia where Jews had a virtual monopoly.

The Jewish Exodus from South Trenton

The Jewish exodus from South Trenton began after World War 1, the movement was westward. First, on West State Street (Gilbert Gold's family moved in 1225 West State Street).

By 1935, one-third of Trenton's Jews maintained their residences in South Trenton. Others generally moved to the Western Section, east of Calhoun Street. Some located their professional offices and lived at the same dwelling.

The Berkley Square Development

Two important factors furthered the development of the western part of Trenton: extension of the trolley lines and the development of Cadwalader Park.

The Horse Car Line

The Horse Car Line defined the westerly flowed of city residents. By 1883, The Horse Car Line extended just beyond Calhoun Street. Thereafter to Prospect Street.

Cadwalader Park

Cadwalader Park development divides into three major chronological periods: Park Planning in 1888–1892, implementation in 1892–1911, maturing maintenance in 1912–1936.

Initially, the wealthy built retreats from the crowded, dirty cities. Often as summer homes, on the rural edges of urban areas. The 'City Beautiful Movement' replicated these pastoral retreats but opened up the beauty of open space to the masses. The progressive era (1890-1914) saw the building of urban parks and park systems throughout in the U.S. Its foremost leader, Frederick Law Olmstead, developed numerous beautiful public parks.

In 1858, he and his partner Calvert Vaux won the competition to design New York's Central Park. For the next fifteen years, Olmsted and Vaux designed Prospect Park and Fort Greene Park in Brooklyn, Washington and Jackson parks in Chicago, and the Buffalo park system.

Then, working on his own, Olmsted planned the park at Mount Royal in Montreal and Belle Isle in Detroit. Olmstead had numerous jobs in New Jersey of which Cadwalader Park may be the most significant. In 1884, his stepson, John C. Olmsted, became his partner. These two men developed the extensive system of Boston parks known as the "Emerald Necklace" two years before they began work on Cadwalader Park.[66]

Figure 33. Scenic Cadwalader Park

By 1890. Olmsted designed Cadwalader Park. Between 1890 and 1892, Olmsted planned Cadwalader Park and its environs for a middle-class residential subdivision. One such development, Cadwalader Place, extended from Overbook Avenue to Lenape Avenue along State St. to the Water Power. Another area, across Parkside Avenue, was Cadwalader Heights. The Olmsted firm devoted much time in the development of Cadwalader Heights from 1905-11.

The "Preliminary Plan" of 1891 became the final version of Frederick Law Olmsted's design for Cadwalader Park. The plan presented signature Olmstead elements including making full use of the landscape qualities, a coherent system of walks and drives (within easy walking or horse carriage distance) and variegated trees and shrubs.

The City converted the Ellarslie mansion into a natural history museum with a restaurant. Citizens donated small animals and birds. City officials also cleared the stables and outbuildings to accommodate a small zoo. (The City added larger animals such as deer, monkeys, and a black bear cub).

Olmstead also planned for sporting facilities, (a baseball diamond, a cricket field and tennis courts). He planted numerous species of shade trees and a sidewalk along Parkside Avenue and the northern border.

In 1912, Olmstead proposed a tunnel to circumvent the canal that impeded entrance to the park from State St. The WPA completed this tunnel in 1932.

Figure 34. Cadwalader Park (1892–1911)

In 1892, a new city administration opposed further major expenditure on public parks. To circumvent this inconvenience, city backers persuaded the Legislature to create a Park Commission. Accordingly, Olmstead scaled down his original plan. In 1911, the Olmstead firm returned to design a Lower Recreation Area to include tennis courts, a running track and two small toilet/locker room facilities.

Cadwalader Park (1912–1936)

The Park became the city center for special events (parades, picnics, reunions, celebrations, strolling, etc. The park advertised itself with displays of annuals flowerbeds spelling "Cadwalader Park" along the canal embankment. The Greenhouse grew assorted annuals.

In 1913, the city built an enclosure for the park deer and converted the Ellarslie mansion and carriage house-to-house monkeys, an animal shed, and aviary; and the Park Commission constructed a bear cage.[67]

In 1897, Cadwalader Place (Berkeley and Carteret Streets) developed into a special residential area for the upper middle-class.

In 1914, the Atterbury Tract developed Atterbury, Delawareview and Colonial Avenues.

Figure 35. Ellerslie Mansion, Cadwalader Park

In 1917, developers extended the West End of the city past the park, extending to Bryn Mawr Avenue, assisted by extension of the new trolley line to Parkside Avenue and Stuyvesant Avenue.

Belleville Mansion, a charming rural retreat dating from Colonial times, stood on a site near where Prospect Street now meets West State. Sir John Sinclair, Revolutionary hero at the Battle of Trenton, owned the mansion.

Further west on State Street stood *Berryville*, formerly the The Mccall-Montgomery Estate. In 1886, Patrick J. Berry developed the fifteen-acre tract into a new residential district of brick-row homes on State Street, West and Avenue, Montgomery Place and North Fisher Place.

Going west of *Berryville*, was the Dickinson estate, *Hermitage*, used as housing for Hessian mercenaries during the Revolutionary War. After the war, the rich and famous frequented this mansion (George Washington, John Adams, Thomas Jefferson, Alexander Hamilton, Livingston, Benjamin Franklin, George Clymer, Marquis de Lafayette, Baron Fredrich von Steuben and other dignitaries).

In 1850, Philemon Dickinson sold the mansion to Edward J. C. Atterbury who developed *Atterbury's Woods*, which, in 1904, became Atterbury Ave.

In 1914, the Atterbury estate developed a semi-detached row house residential area incorporating Atterbury, Delawareview, General Greene and Colonial Avenues.

The Cadwalader family owned the land west of Overbrook Avenue, of one-hundred-and-fifty acres. Dr. Thomas Cadwalader.

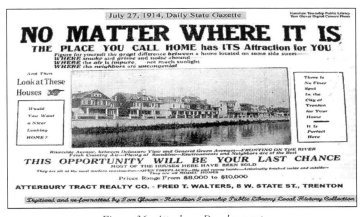

Figure 36. Atturbury Development

Land from the Cadwalader estate, under the supervision Frederick Law Olmstead & Company, developed Cadwalader Place. Again, the extension of the trolley line aided in this development. In 1896, 904 Riverside Avenue presented itself as the first dwelling.

The Berkley Square Development (S. Overbrook to Parkside Avenues) and the Cadwalader and the Hiltonia Developments began in the 1920's.

Berkeley Square (now a Historic District) developed into a well-preserved six-block area known as "Cadwalader Place." Capitalizing on the grandeur of the Park, the developer planned a residential community between 1890 and 1910. This area typified suburban residential planning dominating late nineteenth century cities. The middle class found the best of both urban and rural life. Berkeley Square, approximately 240-acres demonstrated architectural variety, housing quality and planning integrity.

By 1890, John and Richard Cadwalader utilized the land for its developing family residences since 1776. In 1891, the heirs undertook a development called "Cadwalader Place," bordering Riverside, Parkside, Berkeley and Gouverneur Avenues. The City of Trenton purchased some of this land for schools and parks. Edmund C. Hill, a local the promoter and civic leader spearheaded this effort. [68]

Figure 37. Cadwalader Park Drive

To encourage salability, the developers built sewers, utility lines, gas lines, city water, and sidewalks. Hill sold several lots to middle and upper-middle class families eager to escape the highly dense city with its urban issues. He promoted the development as a fine residential suburb.

Amenities included mail delivery three times daily; trolley service, railroad depot, and easy access to police and fire protection. Residents could also walk to schools, libraries, and churches.

Beyond Cadwalader Place was "Lovers' Lane" leading to "Ellarslie," the original name of the Cadwalader Park mansion. As the city grew and traffic on the Belvedere division of the Pennsylvania Railroad increased, there was increased danger of accidents. To avoid these accidents, the City built an entrance in the rear of the park. During the Depression, the City built a tunnel in 1934 on Parkside Avenue to circumvent the hazard.

In 1923, a developer built high-end residential development, known as the Hiltonia Tract.

In 1926, Charles G. Tuenin developed Glen Afton (along the canal, now Rte. #29 to Lower Ferry Road), into three high-end residential sections: Riverview, Hillslope and the Country Club Division.

Figure 38. Cadwalader Height's, off of Cadwalader Park

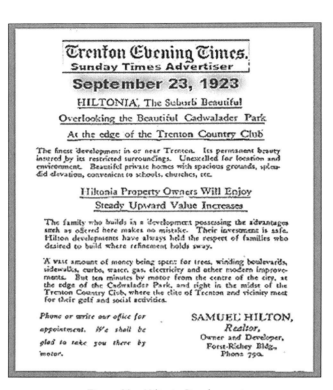

Figure 39. Hiltonia Development

Trenton's Jews, initially residing in South Trenton, sought new homes provided by these new developments.

There was little movement once the Great Depression visited Trenton so most of the housing movement began in the 1920's.

George W. Farlee, a New York stock broker developed the Hillcrest residential tract. The city the park authorities built an outdoor skating 1897, with 1500 skaters on the scene. Across State Street, where Junior High School Number 3 now stands, stood the Y. M. C. A. athletic field.

From 1900 to 1928, the Jewish population in South Trenton decreased 33%. Jews moved Westward into the developing areas (Atturbury Tract, Fisher-Richey, Perdicaris, Berkeley Square, Cadwalader Place, Glen Afton and Hiltonia) to the extent that Jews made up more than 11% of these neighborhoods. Prominent physicians and dentists opened new offices, often living upstairs or in the back of the large house.

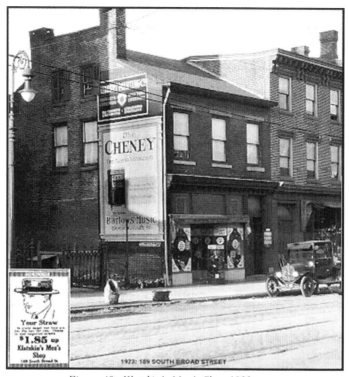

Figure 40. Klatzkin's Men's Shop 1923

Education

Education was the way to economic security. Besides business, education also would produce the many professionals seen in the second generation (the first to speak native English).Those in South Trenton ultimately graduated from Trenton Central High School. Trenton High covered all of Trenton, Hamilton, Ewing, and Lawrenceville. Jewish students distinguished themselves in academics and sports. More so in academics than sports.

In addition to the athletes, Dave Weisberg became the famed soccer coach in 1935. His innovations and motivation created state dominating teams for a decade. Teams still use some of his innovations. Dave alter became an Assistant Principal of Trenton Central High School, giving up his coaching.

For those old enough, the following names are recognizable, representing the best and brightest of the Trenton community. Most of these students remained in Trenton to become pillars of its Jewish and general community.

For first generation Jews, it was difficult adapting to a new culture, new methods of doing business, new interaction between the government and the individual and of course conquering the difficult English language. Some of the second generation developed businesses begun by their immigrant parents. In high school, Trenton Jewish students thrived in the free public schools. Yet they also encountered a caste system because Trenton had a segregated junior high school system until 1943!

Quota systems reared its head in universities, medical schools, law schools, etc. There was almost a total absence of Jews in the banking industry, the securities business, accounting, large law firms, and advertising agencies, among many sectors.

The Professions

Doctors included Dr. Jack Blaugrund, Dr. Jacob Berman (South Trenton, Dr. Bernard Lavine (whose parent owned a sore in South Trenton). The Jewish physicians congregated around North Clinton Avenue and Mulberry Sts. An athlete, Dr. Edgar Fiestal became a physician as well as Dr. Bert Bernstein and Dr. Yale Byer.

Dr. Lester Klempner was a specialist in Pulmonology, treating tuberculosis the many patients who contracted with dread disease. Donnelly Hospital (originally a City TB Hospital), now the Mercer County Geriatric Center, named a building in honor of Dr. Lester Klempner.

Dentists included Dr. Charley Lavine, Dr. Nathaniel Popkin (my Uncle who graduated Dental School at age 19 and had to wait two years before he was eligible to practice at age 21), Dr. Sam Byer, Dr. Nat Byer and Dr. Joes Byer, all of whom shared an office with their physician brother Dr. Mo (Yale) Byer.)

Lawyers included Maurice Gold who apprentices as Katzenbach, Gildea and Rudner. The Rudner was Sam Rudner. His brother Sam also practiced law. Albert Kahn, from one of the older German families has a bustling practice. Sidney Goldmann, Joe Bash and Dave Kravtiz were also attorneys. Sidney

Goldmann tenured as State Librarian, service on the Appellate Court for many years, often filling in vacancies on the N.J. Supreme Court.

Sam Rabinowitz was the clerk for Hon. Sidney Forman, federal Judge (and a national Contract Bridge expert).

The famous optometrist, now in its third generation was Sidney Newman. Sidney's sister was also an Optometrist and as Dr. Larvy.

One accountant, Samuel Klatzkin, C.P.A. (his two sons joined him after they became CPA's) graduated from the Wharton School. He told me that the Wharton School was a breeze because he attended a New York Yeshiva in which he awake at six, ate breakfast, davened, and then attended classes from 9 am to 6pm, both in English and Hebrew. Thereafter, he studied. This routine repeated for five days. He went ONLY a half day on Fridays. He resumed the routine on Sundays. He thought The Wharton School to be child's play.

Trenton's Increasing Jewish Professionals, 1915-1956

In 1915, Trenton's first generation professionals did not reach its percentage in the population. However, the Second Generation and beyond provided Jewish youth the education necessary for the professions.

The table below depicts the percentages of Jews in the professions.

Trenton Jewish Professionals 1915 - 1956

Professions	1915	1935	1946	1956
Accountants	0%	36%	40%	48%
Physicians	6%	13%	14%	24%
Lawyers	12%	25%	29%	37%
Druggists	16%		15%	20%

(Source: Donnelly's Trenton City Directory for raw data)

Figure 41. Albert M. Stark, Esq

In 1915, the Jewish population (5.0 %) barely represented itself in the professions. In 1935, although in the middle of the Great Depression, college educated Second generation Jews accomplished a great deal.

At this point, all professions, held by Jews, except physicians, were overrepresented in the population. Medical Schools overtly discriminated against Jewish applicants. Even, if Jews graduated medical school, they were often denied hospital privileges. Thus, in cities like New York, the Jewish communities built Jewish Hospitals initially to give hospital privileges to Jewish doctors.

Researching Jewish student activity in Trenton High's Yearbook, the Bobashela, Jewish students represented about 4% of the student population in the years between 1922 and 1938. They generally represented 50% of the Bobashela (yearbook) staff. Many of these participants became the next generation's professionals (physician, lawyers, accountants, dentists, etc.). In addition, they became the titans of local business.

This generation, as in other similar communities, disproportionately represented Jews in the professions and in business. The opportunity for education and the motivation to be financially secure was the immigrants' dream for their children.

Figure 42. Physician 1920's

Their appearance in sports was disproportionate only on the tennis team. Otherwise, it was below their percentage in high school. The big exception was that the 1935 and 1936, when Trenton High won the State basketball tournament, with at least three Jews on its twelve-man squad.

The Second Generation also gave back to the Trenton Jewish community. This Generation fleshed start-up organizations with their leadership and became local bastions of national Jewish movements, such as the Jewish National Fund, Hadassah, ORT, Knights of Pythias, Zionist organizations and the Brotherhoods and Sisterhoods of the newer congregations.

Trenton's Jewish-owned textile industry, unlike many cities, did not dominate Jews' occupations. Indeed, in New York, fully 60% of Jews were in the needle trades.

In 1917, the textile industry picked up in Trenton with outside capital mostly from Philadelphia and New York, with Baxter Clothes and Metropol Clothing Factory.

Indeed, although most immigrant Jews did not have skills for the 'new country' businesses, many from textile centers in Lodz, Poland and Bialystock, experienced in the textile business found job awaiting them. However, they did not settle in the Trenton area. Indeed, by 1860, 65 of the 70 garment firms were Jewish-owned in Cincinnati. By 1890, Jewish owned and employed over 50% of Cincinnati Jewish population. Further, data from the 1890 United States Census indicated that 50% of employed Jews worked in the clothing industry.

Along the Passaic River. Paterson and Passaic became textile-manufacturing leaders in the United States by the end of the 19th century.

Indeed, Jewish workers from Bialystock, skilled in the silk textile industry, settled in Patterson, the center of New Jersey's silk textile industry.[69]

Fall of Trenton's Economy

John T. Cumbler's *Social History of Economic Decline: Business, Politics, and Work in Trenton* analyzes the organization of both union and management to trace Trenton's rise to industrial prosperity in the early twentieth century as well as its decline over the past seventy years.

Social History of Economic Decline sketches the earlier world of local industrialists and workers, rooted in the vision of a community of interests shared by pottery owners and workers. Specialized pottery skill caused the encouragement of seeking experienced potters from England. This industry excluded women, blacks, and other unskilled workers. In the 1920's and 1930's, pottery workers unionized but the workers and their employers joined in a mutually beneficial program of high tariffs, high prices, and high wages. However, labor troubles hit the pottery industry very hard in 1923, causing many of the local potteries to merge with national pottery concerns, marking the beginning of the end for civic industrialism. Further, industries like Roebling Brothers began a national corporate structure, with an unhealthy civic consequence for Trenton. Accordingly, the civic synergy between home office and the city lost its luster. [70]

The demise of the pottery industry began after the 1923 strike. After World War II, large industrial amalgamated into national and international companies located outside of Trenton. Factory plants and their jobs left in the 1950's and 1960's. Accordingly, this reduction in workforce detrimentally affected local (Jewish) merchants.

Jewish Trenton's Third Generation +

The 1929 Census records 4,100 Jews. In 1937, a Jewish census study counted 7,191 Jews (about six percent of Trenton's population). Statistics show that thirty-two Jewish philanthropic organizations, existed, including six synagogues. Fifty-nine percent of Jews worked in commerce.

The 1949 and the 1961 censuses documented increases in the professions, which in 1970, probably amounted to nearly 30 percent of all professionals. In 1970, there were 40 Jewish philanthropic organizations, including three Conservative congregations as well as two Orthodox and one Reform congregation. By the beginning of the new millennium, the community within Trenton's city limits had diminished to three congregations, one Orthodox, one Conservative and a Reform congregation.

In 1938, Professor Marcus L. Hansen formulated for students of immigrant history the notion that "what the son wishes to forget the grandson wishes to remember." The third generation regularly meant the approaching dissolution of the ethnic group, which the first generation had formed and with which the second generation had perforce been identified.[71]

Investigating this premise, John Appel found that, unlike Poles or Italians, the third generation only retained their grandfather's religion. Jewish community demonstrated their Jewishness, not by the Orthodoxy of the first generation, but by accommodation, that which other groups achieve by dissolution and disintegration. Far from resisting the process of acculturation, Jews submitted themselves to it but with positive effects. (Somewhat akin to what Jacob Riis hypothesized some 45 years prior). Even before the 1968 race riot, Trenton's Jewish population drifted out of Trenton to the suburbs.

Today, Trenton's Jewish community is a nostalgic memory. The few remaining Jews are well over the age of fifty; children are few. Even the Jewish populations of contiguous Ewing Township and Hamilton Township are moving away to the exurbs.

The Lawrenceville and Yardley-Makefield areas house substantial numbers of Jewish child-raising families.

The burgeoning residential areas center in East Windsor (Twin Rivers Planned Unit Development), West Windsor, Roosevelt, and Princeton.

By 2006, there were only two congregations the city limits, Congregation Brothers of Israel (200 families) and Har Sinai Temple (500 families), both of which were relocating.

Conclusions

Sophia M. Robison, took a snapshot of the Trenton Jewish success story. Using socio-economic data, she concluded that, by 1937 South Trenton residents located to West Trenton scattered throughout Trenton due to their local businesses. Sixty percent of Jews found their vocation in merchandising, more than three and one-half times the ratio of males in the population. Remarkably, Trenton's Jews fell on the high end of similar studies of the proportion of Jews in retail businesses (34% in Passaic, NJ to 60% in Pittsburgh, PA). [72]

Jews represented a higher proportion in the professions than their population numbers. As late as 1915, Jews did not represent their own population percentage in the professions. By 1935, however, the second generation of American-born Jews sought the education that allowed them to become physicians, dentists, accountants and attorneys.

On the other hand, their numbers underrepresented their population as managers in a great manufacturing city. A plausible reason for this disparity is that Jews knew from experience that they did want to be in competition with similarly situated workers. There also were vastly underrepresented in government work and domestic service.

Only twenty Jews in Trenton reported Works Progress Administration employment, probably due to the Jewish institutions taking care of the needy.

Most Jews of married age Jews became married.[73] Accordingly, to some extent, this small Jewish community had an inordinate amount of inter-rations through marriage. Most of the formerly vibrant Trenton Jewish community still lived near Trenton, in the suburbs of Mercer County, New Jersey and across the Delaware River in Buck County, PA.

Centers of non-denominational Jewish organizations Jewish Federation programs (Jewish Family Service, Jewish Community Center, Greenwood House Nursing Home) and the Greenacres Country Club generally locate themselves Lawrenceville-Princeton and Lower Bucks County, PA swath.

Trenton's Jewish Federation merged with another Jewish Federation but still communicates with old Trentonian families with a monthly newsletter (also online).

OUTSTANDING TRENTON JEWISH PERSONALITIES

Judge Phillip Forman

Figure 43. Judge Phillip Forman with friend, Albert Einstein

Born in New York, Judge Forman graduated from Temple University Law School and practice law in Trenton. In 1923, he President Coolidge appointed him United States Attorney for the District of New Jersey (1923-1932). In 1932, President Hoover appointed him federal judge on the United States Court of Appeals for the Third Circuit (New Jersey).

At that time, Judge Forman was the youngest judge (age 36) ever appointed as a District Court Judge. On 1961, he became a senior Judge and continued adjudicate until his death in 1978.

Judge Forman was active in Jewish community as a Trustee of Har Saini Hebrew Congregation.[74]

Judge Sidney Goldmann

Figure 44. Hon. Sidney Goldmann

Hon. Sidney Goldmann, a presiding judge and administrative judge on New Jersey's Superior Court before his retirement in 1971, died Saturday at his home in Trenton. He was 79 years old.

Hon. Sidney Goldmann was a lifelong resident of Trenton, the son of a German Immigrant who helped begin Ahavath Israel.

He graduated from Trenton schools, Harvard in 1924 and Harvard Law School in 1927 whereupon he practiced law in Trenton.

He became city attorney from 1935 to 1939 and acting city manager of Trenton (1943-1944). The next year, he became Executive Secretary to the New Jersey Governor, State Librarian, State Archivist. He was instrumental in New Jersey's Constitutional convention in 1947, which revamped its 1844 constitution. Afterwards, he was the editor of the New Jersey Revision of Statutes.

In 1949, he became Special Master of the N.J. Supreme Court. In 1951, he became a judge of the Superior Court on which he became Presiding Judge form 1954-1971. After retirement, he became a member of the Committee of Supreme Court opinions and headed the State Election Law Enforcement Commission.

He was particularly active in civic affairs. He became the President of Trenton Jewish Historical Society. He was a Trustee of Har Sinai Hebrew Congregation, Jewish Family Service, and Jewish Home for Aged, American Jewish Committee, Trenton Free Public Library, Council on Human Relations, Trenton Symphony Orchestra, among others.[75]

Benjamin Kauffman

Figure 45. Benjamin Kaufman

Benjamin Kauffman received the Congressional Medal of Honor and the Croix de Guerre for bravery in the Argonne Forest in 1918. Kaufman attended Syracuse University on an athletic scholarship, when he volunteered for active duty in 1917.

Blinded by a gas shell and wounded in the right arm, while aiding in the rescue of several of his men, Sgt. Kaufman initially refused medical help but later hospitalized to recover. Sgt. Kaufman 'escaped' from the field hospital, to return his company. Facing a court martial for his unauthorized absence, after he rescued more of his men, knocked out an enemy machine nest and captured several prisoners, Kaufman received awards for bravery from nine foreign governments. (The army decided to drop the military charges.)

After the war, Kaufman lived Trenton. During World War II, he became Director of the War Manpower Commission as well as Commander of the New Jersey Council of the Disabled American Veterans of the First World War and national Vice-commander of the National Legion of Valor. From 1945 to 1959, he became executive director of the U.S. Jewish War Veterans.

He became manager of the N.J. State Employment Service (Trenton), married Dorothy Finkle, a granddaughter of Isaac Levy, a driving force in Trenton early Russian Jewish community and founder of the Talmud Torah.[76]

Sol Weinstein

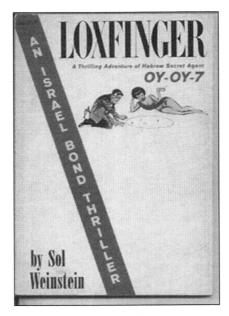

Figure 46. Sol Weinstein's Creation 'Loxfinger'

Sol Weinstein, was born and raised in South Trenton on Union Street. In the 1950's, he wrote for a local newspaper, *The Trentonian*, as an obituary writer. He then embarked in a comedy career. His first great success was as a gag writer for

Joe E. Lewis. His clients were a Who's Who of comedians: Bob Hope, Dean Martin, George Burns, Danny Thomas, Frank Sinatra, Sammy Davis Jr., Bobby Darin, Dom Deluise, Alan King, Jerry Lester, Jackie Kannon and Joe E. Lewis.

He even composed the music and wrote the lyrics to a number titled "The Curtain Falls," which Bobby Darin used to close his act. He also wrote TV scripts "The Love Boat," "Three's Company," "Maude" and "The Jeffersons," as well as contributing to "Laugh-In" and "Dean Martin's Celebrity Roasts."

The zany Weinstein created the characters "Loxfinger," "Matzohball," "On the Secret Service of His Majesty, the Queen" and "You Only Live Until You Die," a parody of the iconic James Bond movies.[77]

Alex Siegle

Dramatist Alex Siegle's family owned a popular delicatessen on Market St. Winner of practically every TV award that existed in early TV, he also received an Emmy for his Broadway production of Death of a Salesman). Siegle, who also directed "One Flew over the Cukoo's Nest," used the Trenton Psychiatric Hospital as its main location. [78]

Sol Linowitz

Trenton's Sol M. Linowitz (December 7, 1913 – March 18, 2005) attended Cornell Law School. He performed legal work for a start-up company, named Xerox Corporation. In lieu of payment for his legal services, he took shares of stock. When the company prospered, he became its Chairman from 1961-66. In 1959, the company produced the first copy machine made available for the commercial market.

Appointed by President Carter as Ambassador for Latin American Affairs, he helped negotiate the treaty returning the Panama Canal to the Republic of Panama.

In 1964, Linowitz and David Rockefeller launched the International Executive Service Corps to help companies in developing nations. Besides being a career diplomat, lawyer, and former chairman of Xerox, he wrote two books, "The Making of a Public Man: A Memoir", and "The Betrayed Profession." In 1998, President Clinton awarded Linowitz the Presidential Medal of Freedom.[79]

Judith Light

Figure 47. Actress Judith Light

Judith Light was born in Trenton, New Jersey. Her parents were Pearl Sue (née Hollander), a model, and Sidney Light, an accountant. She graduated from Doane Academy and Carnegie Mellon University with a degree in drama.

Traveling a long road to stardom, she had a role in *Richard III* at the *California Shakespeare Festival* in 1970. In 1975, she first appeared in the Broadway show, *A Doll's House*. She experienced a dry spell in the late 1970's but rebounded with more than fifty-three roles and two producer credits.

Among her many awards are the Helen Hayes Award for Outstanding Lead Actress, the Tony Award for Best Featured Actress in a Play, the Drama Desk Award for Outstanding Featured Actress in a Play and the Daytime Emmy Award for Outstanding Lead Actress in a Drama Series.

Light is a gay rights activist. She is a trustee of Point Foundation (LGBT). She is also a prominent AIDS activist and played Ryan White's mother in the 1989 TV movie on his life *The Ryan White Story*.[80]

Zalman King (Lefkowitz)

Zalman King Lefkowitz was born on May 23, 1941, in Trenton, where his father was an oral surgeon. He was a champion swimmer in high school.

Figure 48. Zalman King, Actor, Producer, and Director

Dropping out of Grinnell College to work as a commercial scuba diver in California, Zal's rugged handsome looks got him a part on the blockbuster TV series, *Gunsmoke.*

He parlayed this role into 40-more actor parts. However, his fame lay as the writer-director of the Red Shoe Diaries, a made-for-TV movie series tapping into an enormous late night TV market. [81]

Tal Brody

Figure 49. Tal Brody

(See page 52.)

Tony Siegle

Son of a stationery wholesaler, Tony worked for 50 years In Major League Baseball. An original member of that Houston Astro crew in 1965, Tony worked the Astrodome Scoreboard. Going up the ladder, he spent time with the Houston Astros, Philadelphia Phillies, Milwaukee Brewers, San Diego Padres and Montreal Expos/Washington Nationals. He ended his career with the San Francisco Giants in a high executive capacity, specializing in player development.

Figure 50. Tony Siegel at San Francisco Giants Stadium.

A former U.S. Navy Officer, Siegle worked with 24 general managers He possesses three MLB World Series rings. Tony currently consults with for San Francisco Giants.[82]

GENERAL HISTORICAL CAUSES OF
JEWISH IMMIGRATION

Sephardic Immigration

Sephardic (Spanish) Jews, fleeing from the Inquisition in the 1490's, sought haven in Holland, Greece, North Africa and Turkey. Some settled in Dutch possessions in the America's, the Caribbean Islands and Recife, Brazil. Their numbers were small and their number immigrating to North America was in the hundreds. [83]

German-Jewish Immigration in 1820-1880

In 1814-15, German Jews sought refuge in the United States following detrimental changes in governance mandated by Congress of Vienna in 1814-15. By 1816, Germany had experienced waves of Jewish migration from small towns and villages to urban areas. Indeed, in 1816, seven percent of German Jews were city dwellers; in 1866, fifty percent. The second German Jewish wave came from what is now East Germany (Poland, Russia) in pursuit of economic opportunity and to avoid rampant anti-Semitism. The third wave involved those who sought economic opportunity in America. By 1835, German Germans constituted approximately two percent of more than 1.2 million Germans who immigrated between 1820 and 1855. German Jews settled in urban areas and applied their skills to commerce. Single males predominated among Jews. Ethnic German were more likely moved as family units. German Jews sought economic opportunity and religious tolerance. Their aim was emancipate themselves; not assimilate.[84]

Most German Jews came from Bavaria, although some came from the Rhineland, Alsace-Lorraine, the Austro-Hungarian Empire and Posen (a Polish area).

In America, although some German Jews specialized in various crafts (tailors, glaziers, cigar makers, etc.), most were independent business men, a holdover from the old country where the government forbade their owning land.

Accordingly, German Jews, with few exceptions, were not involved in agriculture, as were many other non-Jewish German immigrants.

Americans generally respected German Jewish businessmen, perceived as thrifty and orderly. Although they did not have central political-religious authority like Irish Catholic immigrants, they did establish benevolent societies and synagogues.

Generally, German Jews dominated the secondhand clothing trade, a significant business before mass-production and the resulting wide availability of cheap new clothing. Later they dominated the manufactured clothing business.

Plying their peddling trade, German Jews followed the "Gold rushers" in the West to provide then with household material needs. Levi Strauss, in San Francisco, created the now famous durable jeans with canvas and rivets for Wild West speculators and cowboys. In the South, German Jews opened general stores. [89] Even the few German-Jewish financiers started out as peddlers. [85]

Sociologist Roger Waldinger maintained that rather than attempting to quell business growth among the newcomers, established Americans benefitted from German Jewish enterprise. The Dun Credit agency's (precursor of Dun and Bradstreet) extensive reports on Jewish retailers suggest that native-owned wholesalers dealt freely with Jewish retailers.[86]

Some non-Jewish Americans demonstrated a concern about these Jewish merchants, who conducted their businesses differently. German Jews were did not show transparency in their lending and buying practices. Rather they secured capital from other German Jewish families outside of the normal banking system. As an example, established European Jewish financial houses opened a branch in New York (Oppenheimer, Speyer Banks and Rothschild banks). Many German Jews, having gained enormous success in the retail business, became financiers: Kuhn, Loeb, Lehman Brothers, August Belmont & Co., J. & W. Seligman & Co., Lehman Brothers, Goldman, Sachs & Co., Kuhn Loeb & Co. (Warburg). Jacob Schiff's father represented the European Rothschild bank.[87]

German Jewish Contribution to American Judaism

In the nineteenth century, these German Jews saw most of their Sephardic brethren completely assimilating. These German Jews feared proselytizing, a mission of some Christian sects.

They modeled their religious principles and practices after their Protestant neighbors. Indeed, members in Charleston, SC in 1830's created the "Reformed Society of Israelites for Promoting True Principles of Judaism According to Its Purity and Spirit." In practice, this group encouraged an abbreviated prayer service in the vernacular and regular sermons.

Meanwhile, communal leaders, led by a more traditional German-Jewish religious leader, Isaac Leeser, did in fact adopt some of these Reform innovations (Sunday schools, Jewish hospitals, a religious press and charitable societies).

Leeser published an Anglo-Jewish translation of the Bible; founded the Jewish Publication Society; and edited a Jewish periodical, *The Occident* and *American Jewish Advocate*, which attempted in its pages to unite the diverse voices of the American Jewish community and which fought anti-Semitism. In 1857, Leeser attended the dedication of Trenton's Har Sinai Congregation. In the 1870's, Isaac Meyer Wise, an organizational genius, forged seventy congregations into The Union of American Hebrew Congregations.

Rabbi Wise also established a seminary, Hebrew Union College. This was the first seminary to ordain Rabbi's in America, which like their Protestant predecessors had difficulty attracting educated clergy to American pulpits. Wise also began the publication, *The Israelite.*

The Great Russian Jewish Immigration in 1881-1914

The U.S. Library of Congress estimated that, from 1881 to 1914, more than 1.6 million East-European Jews immigrated to the United States. [88]

Five unique Americans factors eased adaptation for Jewish immigrants: capitalism, science, popular government, secularism, and technological change. The unique character of the United States as a modern society with a general religious toleration enabled adaptation to American norms. [89]

Similar to most areas, Trenton's first-generation of Russian Jewish immigrants struggled to adapt to American (secular) norms. The second generation, rejected their parents' 'otherness' and normalized themselves in a secular society, generally retaining their Jewish cultural heritage.

After World War II, Jews perceived Jewish birth as a matter of course, even if they did not prize it. Neither did they engender negative attitudes towards Judaism, The relationship was best characterized as indifferent. [90]

In 1772 Russia, Prussia, and Austria partitioned the loose confederation of Lithuania-Poland. To Russia, went the northeastern portion (Plotsk and Vitebsk); the Northwestern portion (including Chelm) to Prussia; the Southern Portion (Galicia-including Zamost and Lwow) went to the Austro-Hungarian Empire.

In 1793, Russia, Germany and Prussia partitioned what remained of Poland. In a third 1795 partition, Russia took Kovno, Vilna, Grodno, Novogradok, Brest and Lutsk. Poland ceased to exist.

The three Lithuanian-Polish partitionings materially changed the ethnic configurations of the Russian Europe. Before 1772, Russia housed few Jews. Czarina Catharine II found that she gained four to five million Jews after these partitionings. Her predisposition to reject heretics and Russian citizens' imprecations to curtail economic competition placed economic restrictions for her Jewish subjects. However, the Polish nobles still held on to their rights and privileges in their large estates, often the size of a village.

Catherine replaced the governing Jewish body, the Councils of the Four Lands, with decentralized kehillas (councils) in their place. Kehillas were legal bodies governing the shtetl and collecting taxes for the government. They took orders from the Russian government. The kehillas comprised a political head and a religious leader, the Av Bet Din (head of the rabbinical court). It mediated the domestic and legal activities of the town. The Av Bet Din appointed responsible members of the rabbinate to adjudicate religious and commercial disputes. Further, The Tsarina fashioned the Pale of the Settlement, a restrictive area in which Jews could live with others. There were 50-gubernias (states), each divided into ten districts. The head of the community also provided a school, bathhouses, a ritual pool, and numerous charitable institutions.[91]

The word pale, from the Latin 'palus' means a boundary. The Jewish Virtual Library described the Pale: "The Pale of Settlement included the territory of present day Poland, Latvia, Lithuania, Ukraine and Belorussia. More than 90% of Russian Jews lived in the Pale, which made up only 4% of the territory of Russia. Nevertheless, Jewish population grew from 1.6 million in 1820 to 5.6 million in 1910.

Most Jewish immigrants to the United States had lived in 'Litvakland': Courland (now part of Latvia), Vilna, Grodno and Minsk, in the northern part of the Pale where Jews represented 75% of all Russian Jews who immigrated to the United States. [92]

Even within the Pale, the government discriminated against its Jews; Jews paid double taxes, they were forbidden to lease land, operate taverns or receive a higher education. The government taxed specific Jewish items, such as Sabbath candles and kosher meat.

The Russian government never really wanted another minority. They already had several minorities they unsuccessfully attempted to 'Russify' (Roma, Tatar' Cossacks, Mongols, Khazars, Ruthenians (Ukrainians), Pole, Lithuanians, Latvians, Khaziks, Turks, Rajiv, Kyrgyz, Uzbacks). [93]

Figure 51. Pale of the Settlement

Jewish Immigration to the United States, 1881-1910

JEWISH IMMIGRATION TO THE UNITED STATES, 1881 TO 1910										
Year	Russia	Austria-Hungary	Romania	United Kingdom	Germany	Brit. N.A.	Turkey	France	All Others	Total
1881	3125	2537	30	—	—	—	—	—	—	5692
1882	10489	2648	65	—	—	—	—	—	—	13202
1883	6144	2510	77	—	—	—	—	—	—	8731
1884	7867	3340	238	—	—	—	—	—	—	11445
1885	10648	3938	803	—	1473	—	—	—	—	16862
1886	14092	5326	518	—	983	—	—	—	254	21173
1887	23103	6898	2063	—	780	—	—	—	200	33044
1888	20216	5985	1653	—	727	—	—	—	300	28881
1889	18338	4998	1058	—	758	—	—	—	200	25352
1890	20981	6439	462	—	633	—	—	—	124	28639
1891	43457	5890	854	—	636	—	—	—	561	51398
1892	64253	8643	740	—	1787	—	—	—	950	76373
1893	25161	6363	555	—	1814	—	—	—	429	35322
1894	20747	5916	616	—	1109	—	—	—	791	29179
1895	16727	6047	518	—	1028	—	—	—	871	26191
1896	20168	9831	744	—	829	—	—	—	276	32848
1897	13063	5672	516	—	586	—	—	—	535	20372
1898	14949	7367	720	—	296	—	—	—	322	23654
1899	24275	11071	1343	174	405	5	81	9	52	37415
1900	37011	16920	6183	133	337	—	114	17	49	60764
1901	37660	13006	6827	110	272	—	154	20	49	58098
1902	37846	12848	6589	55	182	—	138	9	21	57688
1903	47689	18759	8562	420	477	—	211	11	74	76203
1904	77544	20211	6446	817	669	8	313	32	196	106236
1905	92388	17352	3854	14299	734	11	173	327	772	129910
1906	125234	14884	3872	6113	979	429	461	479	1297	153748
1907	114937	18885	3605	7032	734	1818	918	306	952	149182
1908	71978	15293	4455	6260	869	2393	635	425	1079	103387[1]
1909	39150	8431	1390	3385	652	2780	690	325	748	57551[1]
1910	59824	13142	1701	4098	705	2262	1388	339	801	84260[1]
Total	1119059	281150	67057	42896	20454	9706	5276	2299	14903	1562800
U.S. Census and Immigration Data										

Figure 52. Jewish Immigration 1881-1910

Figure 53. Immigrant Urchins

The main reason for the Jewish exodus from Russia was economic. Although Russia abolished serfdom (37% of Russia's population) in 1861, this action actually hurt the Jews who were now competitors in the economic marketplace. Further, the Polish nationalists' insurrection of 1863 against Russian domination brought Russian (and Polish) retribution on the Jews, as a scapegoat. The Russian forces confiscated Jewish property. For the Polish noblemen who led the resurrection, Russia confiscated their lands and other property. Some of them were deported to Siberia.

And some, now without means, became economic competitors to the Jews. These developments affected the Jews in two ways: those who had made a living trading with these landowners and noblemen or working as their agents, lost the source of their livelihood. Moreover, these impoverished noblemen moved to the cities, and became competitors to the Jews, even in Pale. Russian economic restrictions on Jewish commerce enabled the noblemen eventually beat out their Jewish competition. Added to these setbacks was pandemic broke out in

Northwestern Russia; bad harvests and the 1871 Odessa pogrom followed by several other pogroms. Nonetheless, Jews could not make a living in the Pale. After the assassination of Tsar Alexander II, the government scapegoated its Jewish population (although there was only one Jew in the conspiracy) by passing 'Temporary' May Laws of 1882.

These draconian laws tightened the noose around Jewish throats. Excess population forced to live in one confined area resulted in overcrowded, blighted areas. One-quarter of the Jewish population was already recorded below the poverty line at that time (which was already low). The anti-Semitic Laws covered the remainder of the Jewish population.[94]

Figure 54. Pogrom in Fury

In addition, thousands of Jews fell victim to anti-Semitic pogroms in the 1870's, 1880's, 1890's, culminating in the Kishinev pogrom of 1905, that traumatized Golda Meir, a 5-year old girl.

The word "pogrom", (Yiddish for destruction) entered the English language between 1880–1885. Generally, a pogrom consisted of a riot that the governmental allowed. Generally, there were fewer than 100 killed, 1,000 injured and much property destroyed. It lasted two-three days.[95]

These pogroms, boycotts and other anti-Semitic discrimination, along with the vulnerability of serving in the Tsar's Army for 25-years, were the tipping points that led to mass immigration to the United States (two million between 1881 and 1914). [96]

American German Jews received shtetl Jews with mixed feelings. The Germans, having immigrated from an Enlightened society in the 1850's had already established their roots in America. In contrast, the Ostjude (Eastern Jew), from a limited obscurantist culture, was a foreign 'greenhorn.' Germans looked with both embarrassment and suspicion on shtetl Jews. [97]

Shtetl Jews generally possessed political autonomy, a questioning approach and dispute resolution methods using rabbinic courts. The shtetl mentality did not intrude in larger community affairs. They blended in like the 'Zelig" character of the cinema. Their attitude was, "We will pay taxes. Leave us alone." [98]

These Jewish communities revolved around the synagogue as the house of prayer, assembly and learning and education. Rabbi's Simeon ben Shetah in 75 B.C.E. and Joshua ben Gamla in 64 C.E., issued decrees providing for compulsory education for males. [99] Such regard for education placed Jews in positions that required literacy and math (non-agricultural occupations). In America, as this story shall account, Jews advanced themselves through their reverence of education. [100]

Figure 55. Forlorn Immigrant

95

In 1891. At the behest of President Harrison, reacting to nativist sentiment against ANY immigrants, Congress established the Weber Commission to discover the reasons why Jewish immigrants poured into the United States. Below are some of its findings.

> *A married (man or woman) who adopts the orthodox Christian faith must sign a declaration to the effect that (he or she) will endeavor to convert (his wife or her husband) to the same faith.*
>
> *Jews on reaching their fourteenth year may be received in the [Christian] Orthodox Church without permission of their parents or guardians.*
>
> *The minister of the interior may allow Jewish children to be converted to any Christian denominations that are tolerated in the Empire, even without the consent of their parents.*
>
> *Every convert to Christianity shall receive a monetary payment from15 to 39 rubles, without distinction of sex, and children half that sum.*
>
> *Only Rabbis certified by the government are allowed to officiate. These Rabbis had to attend Russian-run schools. Basically, they reported to the government.*
>
> *Public prayer and worship may only be held in the synagogues Jews holding services in their houses without permission of the authorities will be punished by law. (Note to Secs. 1o6o and1o61, Vol. XI, Part 1, Law on the Religious Affairs of Foreign Denominations, 1857*
>
> *The establishment of synagogues allowed only in places where there are no less than eighty Jewish houses. The establishment of synagogues is allowed only in places where there are no less than eighty Jewish houses*
>
> *Since 1889, Jews are no longer permitted to serve in the army as bandmasters, and of young Jewish soldiers no greater proportion may be appointed as musicians than one-third of the total number of members of the band. [101]*

The government militarily drafted one of seven Jews compared to one in ten non-Jews. Jews could not become military officers. Military physicians were not allowed Jewish assistants. Those converted prior to draft could be exempted from the draft. If Jews were drafted at age twelve, they would serve an additional six years. To add insult to injury, the government forced the Jewish Community Councils to select potential draftees. Khapers (Jews who received bounties) sought those avoiding the draft.

Russian Revolution of 1905

According to Sidney Harcave, four problems in Russian society converged in a Russian revolution: the agrarian problem, the nationality problem, the labor problem, and the educated class problem.

The agrarian problem affected the peasants and the redistributed of the land. The labor problem dealt with those who worked in the developing factories under a new Laissez-faire capitalism who legitimately felt they were exploited. The educated classes (students of universities, other schools of higher learning, and occasionally those of the secondary schools and theological seminaries) wanted employment commensurate with their educational preparation. The Russian government saw these desires as unpatriotic and subversive.

Russia felt that Jews were a special problem. The government had tried to 'Russify' its Jews with little success. Indeed, those who learned Western nationalism were even more strident in their demand for freedom.

Accordingly, the Russian government devised a set of laws governing Jews separate from the rest of the nation. Therefore, the government treated them with considerable restriction in their economic, social and political lives.

Remarkably although approximately 26% of all immigrants to U.S. returned to their country of origin, only 7% of Jews returned.[102]

Special Taxes Imposed on Jewish Items Caused Much Discontent

Because of the hostile attitude of the Tsar combined with the Russian bureaucracy's attempt to convert its Jews, the Jewish population became very self-reliant. Most became more religiously observant. Some tried assimilation; a few converted; and a few became social revolutionaries.

The Jewish Bund in 1897 became a socialist union of Jews working for the benefit of Jewish workers, following haskala (western thought). It also wanted to change work conditions of both Jews and Russians. In addition, the Bundists (Jewish socialists) made industrial socialism blend into the Jewish tradition in a logician's masterstroke.[103]

When the Bundists found resistance from the owners, the Russian bureaucracy and the Tsars, they had three other options. Zionism provided an outlet to pioneer a hoped-to-be Jewish homeland. However, the backbreaking work, the malaria and other association diseases somewhat restricted volunteers. [103]The second choice was more practical, immigration to the "Golde Medina," the United States. This venture however came with a price as principal Rabbi's as well as the Hebrew-language press, more so than its Russian and Yiddish counterparts, cautioned such adventurers against leaving because they forecasted that Jewish life will be destroyed.

The third consisted of a revolution against the government. (The Revolt of 1905 was defeated.)

Prior to the May Laws, there were stirrings to emigrate from Russia, be it Palestine or another country. Russian officials in charge of Jewish Affairs stated that the "Western frontier" held an escape for the Jews. The Russian-Jewish press screamed this sentiment resulting in the formation of emigrant groups. [104]

Although Jewish religious leaders held fast to their religious traditions and tried to keep their communities becalmed, numerous residents wanted "out."

In New York and other large cities, the established, cultured German Jews did help the newly arrived Russian. However, they did not travel in the same social circles.

By November 1882, the volume of immigrants overwhelmed the Emigrant Aid Societies. Accordingly, Jewish leaders created the United Hebrew Charities to earmark funds to resettle Russian Jewish immigrants.

In Russia, during this time, Jewish children attended only public and private educational establishments in which their parents had a right to residence. Subsidies formerly granted to Jews for public education were repealed. The Weber Commission, a Congressional fact-finding body, noted that, prior to the May Laws, school-age Jews who passed a government test were allowed to enter universities, academies, and other higher educational establishments without restriction.[105]

Figure 56. European Oppression of the Jews

In 1880, the government began to impose a quota of Jews in schooling. (In 1882 the number of Jewish students in the Military Academy for Medicine was limited to 5 percent). After the May Laws of 1882, no Jews were admitted to this academy.

In 1883, the number of Jews in the Mining Institute was limited to five percent; Engineering School, ten percent. In 1887 admitted to the Institute of Civil Engineers – three percent. In 1886, no Jew could attend the Veterinary Institute at Kharkov. In 1887, government restrictions on Jews allowed government schooling: within the pale of Jewish settlement to ten percent; in places outside the pale to five percent. In St. Petersburg and Moscow to 3 percent of the total number of pupils in each school or university. (In some places, the Jews were eighty percent of the total population.). [106] In 1885, Jews were not allowed university scholarships; however, they could receive scholarships from private endowments. The government also placed a ban of the traditional Polish-Jewish monopoly on selling Drinking Alcohol.

The Weber Commission further found that Jewish artisans residing outside the Pale of Settlement could sell only the products of their own work. This restriction looked simple enough, but the authorities restricted the sale of *anything* if the seller did not make the packaging. A licensed guild merchant could not sell goods he had not manufactured and packaged. Jews were liable for more severe punishments than non-Jews for committing the same offenses. [107]

The Weber Commission noted Russian pogroms. Indeed, the Russian government authorized, but not participate, in riots against Jews. Such riots destroyed enormous amounts of property and produced casualties. A pogrom was a mob's uprising against the Jewish population with the government authorities 'looking the other way.'

Prior to the mass murders of the Kishinev pogrom of 1905, pogroms resulted in slight deaths and casualties, with extensive property damage due to the wooden structures' vulnerability to fire. In Balta, in the 1890's, an eyewitness account indicated that a bunch of drunken workers ransacked the Jewish community because their fathers had done this before and they were continuing the tradition. They ransacked, pillaged, set fire to dwellings and stores and generally beat up the vulnerable.

The Priest at the cathedral asked the mob to stop. However, in their drunken stupor, they proceeded with their depredation of the Jewish community. They found refuge at the firehouse and the police allowed them to continue vandalizing. In fact, the police and fire brigades helped the rioters as reconnaissance and spy operatives.

In the Balta Pogrom, the local government actually directed the activities. Forty Jews died: one hundred and seventy wounded, more than twenty cases of rape. Many Jews, particularly the women, became traumatized.

There was considerable damage of houses, dwellings, stores, etc. from fire and looting. Indeed, the aftermath of this pogrom resulted in more than fifteen thousand people without shelter or livelihood.

The property damage and dislocation were great; loss of life and casualties relatively minimal. [108]

Subsequent years did not ease for Russian Jews. In 1884, an anti-Jewish riot occurred outside the Pale of Jewish Settlement, in the ancient Russian city of Nizhniy-Novgorod, which sheltered a small Jewish colony of some twenty families.

Additionally, the government accused its Jews of the new accusation of anarchy and revolutionary doctrines. In response, the government convened the Pahlen Commission in 1894. The Commission faced up to the anti-Semitism of the governing circles and the populace. However, it proposed no effective solution.

The Jewish outflow from Russia to the United States served as a barometer of these persecutions: in 1881 - 8,193 emigrants; in 1883 - 17,497.

The next three years, from 1884 to 1886, this outbound movement sustained its level of 15,000 to 17,000 emigrants annually. During the last three years of that decade, emigration picked up steam, mounting in 1887 to 28,944, in 1888 to 31,256, and in 1889 to 31,889.

In a surprise move, in 1890, the government expelled 15,000 thousand Jews from Moscow (formerly allowed as an exception to the Pale of the Settlement restrictions).

In 1891, to tighten the noose, the government issued a law, threatening criminal prosecution to those Jews who, in their private lives call themselves by names different from those recorded in the official registers. Such restrictions countered the practice of many educated Jews to Russianize their names, such as Gregory, instead of Hirsch; Vladimir, instead of Wolf, etc. It was even forbidden to correct the diminutive names, such as Yosel, for Joseph; Srul, for Israel; Itzek for Isaac, etc. In several cities, the police brought action against such Jews "for having adopted Christian names."

In 1895, the Passport Regulation ordered passports of Jews to be identified as Jews, not Russian citizens.

In 1903, the Pogrom of Kishinev took on a much more invidious meaning. Not only was property destroyed, but also there were numerous casualties.

According to official statistics, 49 Jews lost their lives and more than 500 were injured, some of them seriously; 700 houses were looted and destroyed and 600 businesses and shops were looted.

On October 19 - 20, 1905, riots broke out once more. The pogrom began as a protest demonstration by the "patriots" against the Czar but quickly deteriorated into an attack on the Jewish quarter in which 19 Jews were killed, 56 were injured, and houses and shops were looted and destroyed. Thereafter, there were several more pogroms, both authorized and organized by the government. A much bloodier wave of pogroms broke out from 1903–1906, leaving an estimated 2,000 Jews dead and many more wounded, as the Jews took to arms to defend their families and property from the attackers. The 1905 pogrom against Jews in Odessa was the most serious pogrom of the period, with reports of up to 2,500 Jews killed.

The Tsar reacted severely to quell the civil unrest. Pogroms erupted in 660 towns, mainly in the present-day Ukraine (Southeastern Pale of Settlement). There were no pogroms either in present-day Poland or in Lithuania. [109]

The New York Times described the First Kishinev pogrom of Easter, 1903. The anti-Jewish riots in Kishinev, Bessarabia [modern Moldova], are worse than the censor will permit to publish. There was a well laid-out plan for the general massacre of Jews on the day following the Orthodox Easter. Priests led the mob, and the general cry, "Kill the Jews," was taken up all over the city. The Jews were taken wholly unaware and were slaughtered like sheep. The dead number 120 [Note: the actual number of dead was 47–48 and the injured about 500. The scenes of horror attending this massacre are beyond description. Babies were literally torn to pieces by the frenzied and bloodthirsty mob. The local police did not attempt to check the reign of terror. At sunset, the streets were piled with corpses and wounded. Those who could make their escape fled in terror, and the city is now practically deserted of Jews." Jewish Massacre Denounced," in The New York Times, April 28, 1903.There is also evidence, which suggests that the police knew in advance about some pogroms, and chose not to act. [110]

This series of pogroms affected at least sixty-four areas, including Odessa, Yekaterinoslav, Kiev, Kishinev, Simferopol, Romny, Kremenchug, Nikolayev, Chernigov, Kamenets-Podolsk, and Yelizavetgrad and 626 additional small towns and villages mostly in Ukraine and Bessarabia (contiguous to the Ukraine and Romania). [111]

Romanian Jews

In Romania, a vortex of circumstances also brought the Jewish population to its knees. In 1878, the Treaty of Berlin, concluding the Russo-Turkish War of 1877-78, made Romania an independent state, provided it guaranteed citizenship to all resident people, regardless of creed, full civil, economic and political rights.

Romania, which had precluded Jews from full participation, reconfigured its constitution to comply with the Berlin treaty. However, the government substituted a burdensome procedure: "the naturalization of aliens not under foreign protection should in every individual case be decided by Parliament." This action involved a ten-year term before the government could review the applicant. [112]

By 1912, the government granted citizenship to 4,000 Jews out of 250,000 Jews. Lack of citizenship materially impeded employment and civil rights. In 1893, the Romanian government restricted Jews' opportunity for public school education. In addition, the courts questioned the reliability Jews who refused to take a Christian oath because the government understood that Yom Kippur prayers vitiated such oaths. [113]

An Astounding Similarity: South Trenton and the Shtetl

A striking similarity of Trenton's Russian-Jewish neighborhood and the European Shtetl [where most of Trenton's originated] manifested itself. Similar were the commercial districts; living over their places of business; the relative 'Jewish section of town' with its unique institutions (kosher butchers, kosher bakeries, a mikveh (ritual bath), a Jewish Day School, and several synagogues).

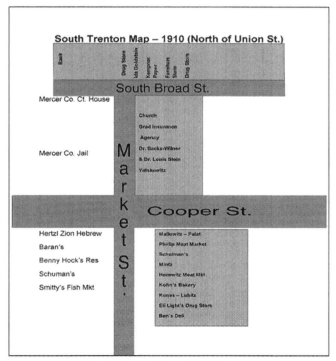

Figure 57. South Trenton, 1910

103

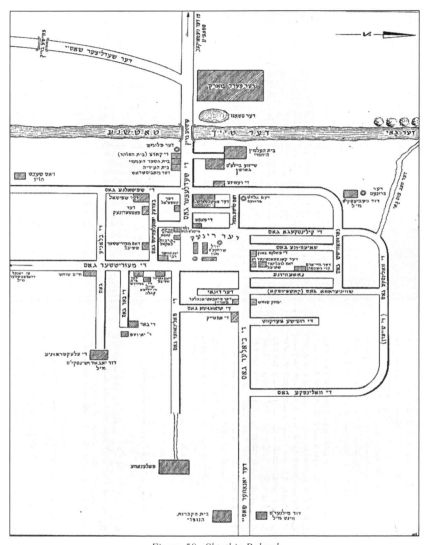

Figure 58. Shtetl in Poland

By 1897, fully one-half of Russia's Jewry lived in large cities (Warsaw, Odessa and Lodz. Housed 5 million Jews). However, the other portion of the population lived in small market towns, called shtetls.

The Jewish Virtual Library reports that the Shtetl was Yiddish diminutive for "shtot" (Yiddish for "town") to imply a relatively small community.

104

Population varied from 1,000 inhabitants to 20,000 or more, many of whom were non-Jews. Polish noblemen owned most of these shtetls. Their old fiefs comprised an agricultural settlement populated by non-Jews and a commercial center generally operated by Jews. The nobles continued to hold legal jurisdiction over his subjects.

Jewish law, supervised by Rabbinical Councils, conducted the rhythms of the shtetl life. There was a school for the young, a ritual bath for the women, kosher meat dealers, etc. The community centered on the synagogue and the family.

Trenton's Russian Jews settled in a commercial area similar to the shtetl. It possessed its kosher butchers, bakeries, mikveh, school and synagogues.

The Characteristic Features of Jewish Migration

Jewish families emigrated as a whole, and Jewish immigrants tended not to return to Europe; twenty-five percent of non-Jews returned. In the year before the First World War, only 5.75 percent of Jewish immigrants returned compared to a full third of other immigrants. Other than peddling, most Jews were not skilled, although some were tailors. Jewish immigration bespoke the yearning for the opportunity to display their value to society, from the intelligentsia to the simple peddler. [114]

Emigrant Preparation and American Ports of Entry

Until 1890, each state in the United States had jurisdiction over admitting immigrants. Five main ports served as disembarkation points for immigrants. New York's Castle Island served as the port for New York City 1830-1892; thereafter Ellis Island served as the main port of entry (1892- 1954); Boston (to 1899); Philadelphia (to 1899); Baltimore (to 1891); and New Orleans (to 1902). A full forty percent of all current U.S. citizens can trace at least one of their ancestors to entry to Ellis Island.

Shortly after the U.S. Civil War, some states started to pass their own immigration laws, which prompted the U.S. Supreme Court to rule in 1875 that immigration was a federal responsibility. [115]

However, the states continued to pass legislation on immigration entry. The Immigration Act of 1891, however, stopped all state incursions into immigration matters. Such immigration procedures became federalized.

Emigration Organizations

German Shipping Encouragement

The Hamburg Shipping Lines built an emigrant's "city" in the port area for refuges to accommodate 5,000 people. Facilities included a kosher canteen and a synagogue. Local Jewish organizations also assisted those Jews awaiting sailing.

Trenton's Jews indirectly benefited from the German Ship lines. However, they were direct beneficiaries of the following organization who arranged their emigration and relocation. In 1891 in London, Baron Maurice de Hirsch, a German Jewish banker, devised an idea that Jews should become agriculturalists, something denied in Europe.

Accordingly, he established a society to benefit those who wished to become farmers. He and the Russian government agreed to relocate Jews up to 3,250,000 Jews emigrating over a 25-year time period to Argentina. Baron de Hirsch also sponsored sixteen agricultural developments in the United States. [116]

Figure 59. Hamburg RR Station

In England, the London Board of Guardians helped; in Paris, Alliance Israélite Universelle; in Germany, the Hilfsverein der Deutschen Juden.

In 1907, the Jewish Territorialist Society established in Warsaw to relocate European Jews wherever they would be accepted, not exclusively Palestine.

However, it closed its doors the next year, although the organization itself continued.

In 1909, the Kiev Jewish Emigration Society redirected Jewish emigration outside overpopulated large cites (New York, Philadelphia, Baltimore, Boston and Chicago) to the southern and southwestern states of North America, where there seemed to be more economic opportunity.

It assisted the Jewish emigrant from departure from Russia to establish a new location in another country to the extent that they no longer need assistance.

Supported by well-to-do American German Jews, one of their experiments was immigration to Galveston, Texas.

Figure 60. Border Police Checking Immigration Papers

This experiment was a middling success, Jewish immigrants numbered. Altogether, 12,000 Jewish immigrants arrived at Galveston port from 1907 to 1913. By 1913, the threatened competition to nativists and the 'strange' religious rituals. Jews exacted political retribution from the Texan communities. [117]

American Organizations Assisting New Immigrants, HIAS

When the Jewish refugees arrived in America, The Hebrew Immigrant Aid Society (HIAS), heavily supported by Jewish philanthropists, provided shelter on Ward Island in the New York harbor and in Greenpoint, in Brooklyn. The agencies also helped to resettle families.[1] The Hebrew Immigrant Aid Society had offices in Hamburg, Berlin, Antwerp and London to help immigrants find employment in New York and New Jersey and established agricultural colonies in other states.

Overwhelmed by the enormous volume of refugees, HIAS gave way to the United Hebrew Charities, New York's organization for Jewish assistance. As the immigrant population cascaded, even the United Hebrew Charities developed a specialized agency (The Hebrew Immigrant Aid Society - HIAS) specifically for the assistance of Jewish immigrants, in 1885.

HIAS advocated for those Jews, who were initially screened out of the immigration process, arguing before the US Boards of Special Enquiry to prevent deportations. It lent needy Jews the $25 landing fee, and obtained bonds for others guaranteeing their employable status. Many Trentonians received help from this organization. [118]

The Jewish Colonization Association

Baron Maurice de Hirsch saw fellow Jews in need of assistance and directed his philanthropic efforts to assist with emigration as soon as possible. His negotiations with the Russian government provided for the allowance of 15,000 emigrating Jews until Russia was 'rid' of its 3.2 million Jews.

Chartered in London in 1891, it took the name the Jewish Colonization Association (JCA or ICA). However, de Hirsch's scheme to buy land in Argentina and resettle Russia's Jewish population ran in to snags. Primarily, Jews did not want, nor were equipped for the farming life. Nonetheless, by 1891, ten thousand Jews dispersed over six Argentinian colonies. By 1905, only 15,000 Jews had immigrated to Argentina.

A popular option was to immigrate to the United States. In 1891, United States absorbed more than 100,000 immigrants.

Many more arrived in seriatim until 1914 at a rate of 30,000 to 35,000 per year.

In 1904, Dr. Theodore Hertzl visited Russia to encourage his Zionist movement. In the same year, Dr. Hertzl found that his Uganda initiative in which Britain promised a safe land for Jewish refugees in Africa met with stiff resistance at the Seventh Zionist Congress in Basle.

After the Russian delegation walked out of the convention, the Zionist movement split. The Zionists aimed efforts was to settle in Zion (Palestine). The Territorialists aimed to immigrate to any safe haven.

Pogroms continued during the Russo-Japanese War of 1904-5. Even though a disproportionate percentage of Russia's people (30,000 Jewish soldiers) appeared at the front, the Russians continued to persecute its Jews.

In 1905, outside the Pale, the Jewish Self- Defense League formed. World opinion forced the Russian government to prosecute the malefactors of the Kishinev Massacre and the Homel pogrom. When only 36 of the 600 indicted were convicted, due to the preclusion of cross-examination by the Jewish attorneys, these Jewish attorneys walked out, causing another stain on Russian 'justice' and more strain on Russian-Jewish relations.

APPENDIX 1

Original Stores in South Trenton, 1910

Bakers
Kohn's
Kunes's
Kramer's

Kosher Butchers
Cattle dealer – Isaac Dohen
Wholesale – Myron Cohen
Cow Dealer – Sharky Rosenthal
Hafetz - David Hafetz passed on his store to his son(s) Joseph and Frank Hafetz
Katzeff and Weiner
Morris Stern
Kalman
Horowitz
Liberty Meat Market

Produce
Silverstein's – Fruit and Produce
Fish and Produce – Solomon Cohen
Grocer – David Cohen

Meat and Produce – Maurice Finkle
Produce Wholesalers – Litowitz and Son, Decatur St.
Grocery Stores
George Levie
Jacob Levie
Samuel Levin
Feldman's
Wineberg's

Fish (including live carp)
Smitty's – Sam Smith

Barker's - Fish Market
Chickens
Balitz Chickens
Feigman's chickens

Tires
United Tires - Irving Cohen
Izzy Richmond
Junk Dealers
Harvey Cohen
David and Jack Introligator
Sam Saperstein

Restaurants
Charles Levie
Benny Hock
Café – Heifel Cohen
Spiegel's Furniture

Small Department Stores
Normal Department Store – Swamp Angel (Isaac Finkle)
Finkle's Dry Good's – Willow and Spring Sts. (Sam Finkle)

Store Owners
Klempner's
Max Nabutovsky
Sadie Cohen
Kravitz'
Mercer Paint and Paper Company - Marcus-Nitzburg family, owned
(Milton) Palat's Furs

APPENDIX 2

Jewish Cemeteries

Jewish cemeteries in the Trenton New Jersey area range from private (Jewish only) cemeteries to consecrated Jewish ground within larger non-sectarian cemeteries. The oldest cemeteries are Jewish only. Jewish only cemeteries, several congregation and small lodge cemeteries, are located near Cedar Lane in Hamilton Township. Short fences with concrete footpaths surround these cemeteries. They are not large, and are near capacity. The newer cemeteries are dedicated Jewish grounds within larger public cemeteries in both Hamilton and Ewing Townships. These have black-topped roads for vehicles; the Jewish sections are open without any enclosures. Genially, Jewish funerals were under the direction of Poulson & Van Hise, Schutzbank Chapels, Ewing Township and Orland's Ewing Memorial Chapel, Trenton.

Adath Israel Cemetery: Greenwood Cemetery, Hamilton Township, and Forest Lawn Memorial Park, Ewing Township.

Brith Sholem TCL 39: Pitman Avenue, Hamilton Township.

Brothers of Israel (Achainy B'nai Israel) Cemetery: Liberty and Vroom Streets, Trenton, New Jersey, and Cedar Lane, Hamilton Township. The Vroom and Liberty Streets cemetery is fully enclosed with a wrought iron fencing with occasional brick/stone pediments. The name of the congregation is on the gate that is in the center fronting Vroom Street. No roadways for vehicles but there are paved walkways. In 1913, the synagogue established an auxiliary cemetery at Cedar Lane and Clover Avenue, in Hamilton Township. Cemetery records are maintained by 530 Washington Crossing Rd, Newtown, PA 18940-2906.

Congregation of the People of Truth (Anshe Emes) Cemetery: Ridge Avenue and Cedar Lane, and Clover Section, further east on Pitman Avenue, Hamilton Township. The first cemetery at Ridge Avenue and Cedar Lane, fronting on Cedar Lane, has a locked vehicular gate, but no paved roads. The cemetery is surrounded by chain-linked fencing and is all grassy without walkways. Stones are newer and medium-size.

The second cemetery further east and entered from Pitman Avenue is enclosed by a large wrought iron fence with a gate with Anshe Emes in Hebrew and a sign "People of Truth Cemetery Association-Clover Section" to the right of the gate. A single black-topped foot path goes through the center from front to rear. The stones are medium to large with the larger stones often having long Yiddish inscriptions. People of Truth is now merged into Poale Emes.

People of Truth, Clover Section on Cedar Lane, has one Jewish burial (name unknown) in the Chambersburg section of Trenton. Source: Shari Myers, Congregation Ahavath Israel Cemetery: two cemeteries on Pitman Avenue off Cedar Lane, and Ahavath Israel-Workman's Circle Br. 90 on Ridge Avenue, Hamilton Township. The two burial grounds with main entrances from Pitman Avenue cover the block over to Clover Avenue. There are also entrances on Clover Avenue. The two cemeteries are separated by the cemeteries for Workmen's Circle Br. #90 and Brith Shalom TCL 39 and Trenton Young Judea. A third burial ground Ahavath Israel-Workman's Circle Br. 90 is on Ridge Avenue. Ahavath Israel Congregation, 1130 Lower Ferry Road, Ewing. Congregation Workers of Truth (Poale Emet) Cemetery: Cedar Lane and Pitman Avenue, Hamilton Township. A chain-linked fence surrounds cemetery, with no roads within. Last known address, Congregation Workers of Truth, 832 West State, Trenton. Ewing Cemetery/Crematorium: 78 Scotch Road, Ewing Township. .Har Sinai Section.

Young Judea Section-more recent burial ground.

Fountain Lawn Memorial Park (Adath Israel).

Fortitude Benevolent Association: Pitman Avenue, Hamilton Township.

Fountain Lawn Memorial Park: 545 Eggert Crossing Road, Ewing Township.. Non-sectarian with consecrated Jewish section. One black-topped road through center. Adath Israel Section is marked with engraved large gray marble obelisk. Dedicated in 1953. Greenwood Cemetery: 1800 Hamilton Avenue, Hamilton Township. Non-sectarian with consecrated Jewish section. Blacktopped roads. Well-maintained. No enclosures marking Jewish section. Adath Israel Section--Closer to Greenwood Avenue than Har Sinai's area. Flat markers, small markers and medium markers. Includes large family plots. Har Sinai Section.

Har Sinai Cemetery: Vroom and Liberty Streets, Trenton, and Ewing Cemetery, 78 Scotch Road, Ewing Township. Har Sinai was the first German synagogue starting around 1860 with services in German and Hebrew. The Har Sinai Cemetery Association was organized at a meeting held November 19, 1857, prior to the start of their first services. In that same year, a lot was purchased for burial purposes at the corner of Vroom and Liberty Streets,

Trenton, New Jersey. Chevra Bikur Cholim was founded in 1876/1877 with Herman Rosenbaum as president. The Vroom and Liberty Streets Har Sinai Cemetery have old small-sized stones (pre-1900), few in number with many illegible due to weathering and moss growth.

Knights of Pythias: Clover Avenue off Cedar Lane, Hamilton Township. Cemetery is surrounded by chain-linked fence without any roads within. Area is grassy with flat, small and medium markers.

Trenton Young Judea Association: Pitman Avenue, Hamilton Township, and a more recent burial ground at Ewing Cemetery.

Workmen's Circle Cemetery Br. #90: Pitman Avenue, Hamilton Township. The Workmen's Circle began its activities in 1924.119

APPENDIX 3

Jewish Organizations

1857 Har Sinai Cemetery Association
1860 Har Sinai Hebrew Congregation of the City of Trenton
1877 Chebruh Buker Cholin (Visting the Sick Society)
1883 Hachaino Benai Israelites of Trenton New Jersey
1885 The Children of Israel Cemetery Co.
1888 Young Hebrew Association of the City of Trenton
1891 Chore Husha Hemess (People of Truth Synagogue)
1891 The Young Men's Hebrew Pleasure Club of Trenton, N. J.
1893 Har Sinai Charity Society
1894 Beneficial Society
1895 South Trenton Republican Club
1895 The Trenton Hebrew Beneficial Society
1897 The Congregation of the Sons of Jacob
1899 The Progress Club of Trenton
1900 Chevre Ansha Ames (People of Truth Synagogue)
1901 Hebrew American Republican Club
1906 The ZES Association The ZES Association (for advancement of Zionism
and Education, Sociability)
1907 The People of Right (Decatur St.)
1908 Progressive Republican Club of the City of Trenton
1908 Keneseth Israel (Union St.)
1909 Congregation of Ahavath Israel of Trenton, NJ
1910 Young Men's Hebrew Association
1910 United States Grand Lodge of the Independent Order Ahavath Achin
1913 Synagogue of the Ahavas Sholom (South Warren St.)
1913 Hebrew Butchers Protective Association
1913 Young Men's Hebrew Social Club
1915 Elysian Club
1916 Young Judaea Association, of Trenton, N. J.(Youth org. to promote
Zionism, Education, and Sociability)
1916 Young Men's Hebrew Association of Trenton, N. J.
1920 Congregation Synagogue Workers of Truth
1921 South Trenton Ladies Blkur Chalim Society
1923 Adath Israel Congregation of Trenton., N. J., 18 S.(Stocton St.)

1924 Workingmen's Circle, Branch, Number 'Ninety
1925 The Progress City and Country Club, Trenton, N. J. (Change name from "The Progress Club of Trenton NJ and amend purpose to "maintain a city and country club house, social intercourse and recreative exercise.
1925 Workmen's Circle, Branch 77
1927 American Hebrew Beneficial Loan *Association*
1930 Hebrew Free Loan Association of Trenton, N. J. (Change of name)
1934 Trenton Young Judea Association of Trenton, N. J.
1935 Jewish Ledger, Inc.
1937 Jewish Family Welfare Bureau (conduct work of charitable nature among persons of Jewish faith social work and welfare, 18 South Stockton St)
1938 Greenacres Country Club
1938 Young Judea Association, of Trenton, N. J.
1938 Brith Rambam (social intercourse, general culture, South Logan Ave.)
1938 Ahavo Torah Achvo Sorority (advance ideals of love, sociability and learning) 18 South Stockton St.
1938 Trenton Ladies Sick Benefit Society (dissolved shortly thereafter)
1939 Trenton Post #156 Jewish War Veterans, Memorial Building
1939 Trenton Hebrew Sheltering Association
1945 Jewish Peoples Fraternal Order Branch #77 (relief for members, burial funds
1945 Hebrew Free Burial Society of Trenton, N. J.
1949 Greenacres Holding Company
1949 Jewish Community Center of Trenton (Change name from "Young Men's Hebrew Association of Trenton, NJ"
1951 Brotherhood of Rabbi Jacob, further Jewish Education, 110 Lamberton Street
1951 Trenton Jewish Community Center Association to encourage and support, Jewish organization, 162 West State Street)
1954 Department of New Jersey, Jewish War Veterans of the United States of America Convention
1955 American-Israeli Lighthouse, Inc.
1959 People of Truth Cemetery Association
1962 Adath Israel Cemetery Association
1962 Ritualatorium Association (charity)
1963 The Foundation of the Jewish Federation of 'Trenton (to receive and administer funds for chartable porpoises
1963 Greenacres Foundation

Unincorporated Organizations 1857-1963

A. Trenton Literary Society,	1882
B. Eagle Educational Club	1893
C. Hebrew Educational Society	1900
D. Brith Achim	c. 1902
E. Independent Order Sons of Jacob, Capital City Lodge 64	1908
F. Mizrachi	no date
G. Dr. Syrkin Branch 94, Jewish Nationalist Workman's Society	1914
H. Poalei Zion	no date
I. Pioneer Women	1926
J. Junior Hadassah	1927
K. Hadassah Women	1932
L. Trenton Zionist District	c. 1932
M. Business and Professional Women's Hadassah	c. 1940
N. International Workmen's Order ca. 1929	
O. Emma Lazarus Women's Auxiliary	no date
P. New American Club	1921
Q. Brith Sholom Lodge	1906
R. Hebrew Ladies Auxiliary of Deborah 1925	
S. Young Wowen's Hebrew Association (YWHA).	1915
T. Sunshine Welfare Club	1915
U. Trenton Yiddishe Veit (newspaper)	1909
V. Die Trenton Vachenblatt (newspaper)	
W. Ivriah (sisterhood) c. 1928	
X. Sphinx Club	c. 1921

Source: Rabbi Paul Teicher, The Jewish Organizations Incorporated In Mercer County New Jersey 1857—1964, consulting Their Incorporators (Farmingdale New York, Farmingdale Jewish Center, 1967. Source from Incorporations, Religious Societies, Volumes A through C. (Vol. C was current in 1964); Merzbacher, John S., Trenton's Foreign Colonies. Trenton: Press of Beers & Frey, 1908; Paul Teicher, "The Dr. Herzl Zion Hebrew School, a History, 1883-1964," appearing in the School's Scholarship Dinner Journal, January 31, 1964, Trenton, N. J.; and interviews with Mr. Leon Kasman, in 1966.120

APPENDIX 4

Surnames

Aaron	Davis	Introligator	Rosenthal
Abramson	Dean	Isaac	Roth
Abrams	Deitz	Kaplan	Rotmon
Abromovitz	Deskin	Kaufman	Roth
Adler	Diamond	Klein	Rothstein
Albert	Disbrow	Klempner	Saken
Aronis	Diskin	Kolman	Schwartz
Barker	Dushman	Koplion	Seigel
Beck	Eckstein	Lavine	Seitlein
Berger	Epstein	Lefkowitz	Salway
Berkelhammer	Farber	Levie	Shein
Berkowitz	Finkel	Levin	Siegel
Berman	Finkle	Levine	Silver
Bernstein	Fisher	Lewishn	Silvers
Berkowitz	Garb	Miller	Silverstein
Berman	Gans	Millner	Simon
Bernstein	Gerofsky	Moschewitz	Snyder
Black	Galinsky	Moskowitz	Stark
Blaugrund	Gold	Naar	Stein
Block	Goildberg	Nabutovsky	Urken
Bloom	Green	Newman	Vogel
Borstein	Greenberg	Nitzberg	Wacks
Brodner	Gross	Oppenheim	Warren
Brooks	Gutstein	Papier	Weinberg
Brown	Halapin	Patinsky	Weissman
Budson	Harris	Peitzman	Weiss
Byer	Hafetz	Phillips	Wirtshafter
Caplan	Heller	Platt	Wolf
Chorosh	Hirsch	Popkin	Wolfberg
Cohen	Hirschfield	Rappaport	Wolff
Cohn	Hirsh	Rednor	
Cooper	Horowitz	Robinson	

APPENDIX 5

Professionals

Fitzgerald's City Directory – 1935

Physicians

Dr. Jacob Berman

Dr. Yale Byer

Dr. Mo Byer

Dr. Eckstein

Copeland

Dr. Lester Finkle

Dr. Arthur Randelman

Dr. Kagan

Dr. Ivy Smith

Blaugrand

Dr. Sam Freidman

Irv Poyas

Dr. Percy smith

Dr. Drezner

Dr Barney Lavine

Dr. Epsten

Dr. Sacks-Wilner

Dr. Zimskind

Dr. Levin

Ed Feistal

Dentists

Miller

Ben Vine

Herman Moss

Greenwald

Sam Byer

Norman Vine

Nat Popkin

Ben Miller

Sacks-Wilner

Stein

Optometrists

Ed Fier

Saloons

Chick Bash

Murf Cohen

Mugsy Resnick

Jumbo Saperstein

Orville Cohen

BIBLIOGRAPHY

Adams, Ruth R., Ph.D., Professor and Associate Dean Emerita of the City College of New York, Immigrant Pioneers, The Jewish Magazine, May 2011.

Alpern, Ed, http://trentonjewishproject.blogspot.com/. Accessed June 5, 2012.

Alpern, Ed, https://picasaweb.google.com/TrentonJewishProject/JEWISHTRENTONPHOT OS#slideshow/5574362035713510514. Accessed January 5, 2012.

American Jewish Yearbook, Philadelphia, Jewish Publication Society (1907_8, 1920. 1930, 1937, 1942 and 1949).

American Jewish Committee Publications, (New York).

The Americanization of the Synagogue, 1820-1870, American Jewish History, Volume 90,(Number 1, March 2002), pp. 51-62 | 10.1353/ajh.2003.0012 traces the development of American Judaism as a process of indigenous religious innovation.

Appel, John, "Hansen's 'Third-Generation Law' and the Origins of the American Jewish Historical Society," Jewish Social Studies, XXIII, No. 1 (Jan. 1961, 321).

Bachin, R., Al Samet's Deli on Miami Beach. In Travel, tourism, and urban growth in greater Miami: Immigration and migration. Retrieved February 21, 2009, from http://scholar.library.miami.edu/miamidigital/ migration3.html.

Avraham Barkai's Branching Out (1994) and Naomi W. Cohen's Encounter with Emancipation: The German Jews in the United States, 1830-1914 (1984) describe continuities and discontinuities between the American and German Jewish experiences, while Leon Jick,

Baron, Salo W. The Russian Jew under Tsar and Soviets (New York: MacMillan Publishing Company, 1976).

Beginning of an Industrial Giant, Accessed   September 3, 2014. http://www.state.nj.us/counties/mercer/about/history/industrial-giant.html;

Bender, Eugene I. And George Kagiwada, Hansen's Law of "Third-Generation Return" and the Study of American Religio-Ethnic Groups N 1938, Professor Marcus L. Hansen ... www.jstor.org/stable/274020. Accessed September 4, 2014.

Berkin, Carol, Christopher L. Miller,, Robert W. Cherny, & James L. Gormly,, Making America A History of the United States, Third Edition, (Boston: HUGHTON Mifflin Co., 2008).

Berkin et al, Making of American, fifth edition, (Boston: Houghton Mifflin (now Wadsworth, 2005).

Becker, Sandra Hartwell & Ralph L. Pearson, The Jewish Community of Hartford, Connecticut, 1880-1929, The American Jewish Archives, http://americanjewisharchives.org/publications/journal/PDF/1979_31_02_00_becker_pearson.pdf. Accessed June 12, 2012.

Bender, Eugene I. and George Kagiwada. Hansen's Law of "Third-Generation Return" and the Study of American Religio-Ethnic Groups, Phylon (Clark Atlanta University, 1960), Vol. 29, No. 4 (4th Qtr. 1968), pp. 360-370.

Billington, Ray Allein, The United States American Democracy in World Perspective (NY: Rinehart & Company Inc., 1947)

Birmingham, Stephen, Our Crowd: The Great Jewish Families of New York, (Syracuse. NY: First Syracuse University Press 1996).

Bloom, Meyer, Accessed April 17, 2014.
http://www.jewsinsports.org/profile.asp?sport=basketball&ID=106.

Encyclopedia of JEWS in Sports, by Bernard Postal, Jesse Silver, and Roy Silver (New York: Bloch Publishing Co., 1965), The Official NBA Encyclopedia: Third Edition, edited by Jan Hubbard (New York: Doubleday, 2000); Robert L. Mendell, Who's Who in Basketball (New York Times, March 17, 1938).

Blumenfeld, S. (2008). The Spertus institute of Jewish studies. Retrieved August 8, 2009, from http://www.jewishvirtuallibrary.org/jsource/judaica/. Accessed July 25, 2012.

Brautbar, Shirli, "Not just ladies that lunch": Hadassah and the formation of American Jewish identity. ProQuest Dissertations and Theses; 2005; ProQuest Dissertations & Theses (PQDT).

Brody, Tal, http://www.tutorgig.info/ed/Tal_Brody. Accessed April 11, 2014.

Borowitz, Eugene B. Reform Judaism Today (New York: Eugene B. Borowitz.).

Borowitz, Eugene B. Liberal Judaism. (New York: Union of American Hebrew Congregations, 1984).

Cadwalader Park, http://www.trentonnj.org/PARKS/CadwaladerPark.html. Accessed April 15, 2013.

Cadwalader Park Master Plan,
http://www.trentonnj.org/PARKS/CWP_Plan_Chapter3.html Accessed April 15, 2013.

City Museum T Ellerslie, http://www.ellarslie.org/about_pottery.htm. Updated 03/26/08. Accessed May 11, 2012.

City of Trenton, New Jersey. Charter and Ordinances. (Trenton, NJ: John L. Murphy Publishing Co, 1903).

Changing Community: A Study of the Jewish Community of the Greater Trenton Area, Jewish Federation of Greater Trenton, In Cooperation with Mallach-Hinden & Associates, (Alan Mallach and Edward Hinden), August 1965.

Chy Lung v. Freeman (92 U.S. 275, 1875).

Cohen, N. W. (1972). Not Free to Desist: The American Jewish Committee 1906-1966. (Philadelphia: The Jewish Publication Society of America, 1968).

Sharonne Cohen, Eruv, http://www.myjewishlearning.com/practices/Ritual/Shabbat_The_Sabbath/In_th e_Community/Eruv.shtml. Accessed August 12, 2012.

Cookson, C. Encyclopedia of Religious Freedom. (London: Taylor & Francis, 2003).

Cumbler, John T., Social History of Economic Decline: Business, Politics, and Work in Trenton. (New Brunswick and London: Rutgers University Press, 1989.) xii, p 302.

Diner, Hasia, A Time for Gathering: The Second Migration, 1820-1880 (Baltimore, MD: Johns Hopkins Press, 1992). Dorff, Elliot. A Living Tree: The Roots and Growth of Jewish Law. (Albany: State University of New York Press, 1988).

Dorff, Elliot. "Autonomy vs. Community: the Ongoing Reform /Conservative Difference" in Conservative Judaism (1996), pp.: 64-68.

Dubnow, Simon,, History Of The Jews In Russia And Poland: From The Death Of Alexander I Until The Death Of Alexander III, Vol. II, (1825-1894). Philadelphia: The Jewish Publication Society of America 1918. A Project Gutenberg EBook, http://www.gutenberg.org/author/Simon_Dubnow.Accessed September 6, 2012.

"Eating and being: what food means," ed. Harriss-White, B. and Sir R. Hoffenberg, eds., Food. (Oxford: Basil Blackwell, 1994) pp 102-115.

Einhorn, Deborah Skolnick, Power of the Purse: Social Change in Jewish Women's Philanthropy, February 2012. Dissertation, Brandeis University, MI Number: 3494428.

Elazar, Daniel, The Covenant Tradition in Politics, Volume 3, Chapter 1 (Jerusalem: Jerusalem Center, for Public Affairs, The Covenant Tradition in Politics, Volume 3, Chapter 1, 1998).

Elazar, Daniel, Jerusalem Center for Public Affairs. Paper presented at the Conference on Geopolitics and Globalization in a Post-Modern World, 25-30 January 1998, Haifa University, Haifa, and Ben-Gurion University, Beersheva, Israel. http://www.jcpa.org/dje/articles3/sci-geo.htm. Acc. October 10, 2012.

Eliach, Yaffa, There Once Was a World: A Nine-Hundred-Year Chronicle of the Shtetl of Eishyshok, (Boston: Little, Brown and Company, 1999).

Encyclopedia Judaica, http://www.cf.jiddisch.org/kehilot/moldova/pogrom-kishinev.htm. Accessed August 14, 2012.

Einhorn. Deborah Skolnick February 18, 2010. http://ejewishphilanthropy.com/dual-loyalities/.Accessed October 16, 2013.

Ettinger S., "Serkele" and "Der Fetter in America," reprinted in S. Ettinger, ed. M. Weinreich, Wilno, 1925, and idem, Inyzo2py) ply, ed. M. Erik, Kiev, 1935.

Gordis, Robert, Josiah Derby, and National Academy for Adult Jewish Studies. Conservative Judaism: An American Philosophy. (NY: Behrman House, 1945).

Milton Feinberg's Papers on Early Trenton Jewry, Trenton Free Public Library. Accessed February 2012.

Fels, Tony, "Religious Assimilation in a Fraternal Organization: Jews and Free-masonry in Gilded-Age San Francisco.," American Jewish History, June (1985), pp. 369-403.

Fishman, Sylvia Barack, Transformations in the Composition of American Jewish Households [NY: American Jewish Committee (AJC), Jerusalem Center for Public Affairs (JCPA)], 2010).

Foster Commission Report of 1892, http://www.angelfire.com/ms2/belaroots/foster.htm. April 1, 2014.

Robert I. Friedman, Inconvenient Truth, Village Voice, July 9, 2002.

The Galveston Movement - My Jewish Learning, Accessed January 2, 2016, www.myjewishlearning.com/.../the-galveston-movement.

Gartner, Lloyd P., Nezhin in Philadelphia: The Families and Occupations of an Immigrant Congregation,. Jewish History, Vol. 8, No. 1/2, The Robert Cohen Memorial Volume (1994), pp. 229-253. Accessed http://www.jstor.org/stable/20101199.

Garber, Lloyd P., History of the Jews of Cleveland: Western Reserve Historical Society in cooperation with the Jewish Community (Cleveland, OH., Federation of Cleveland, 1987).

Harry Gerofsky's Papers on Early Trenton Jewry, Trenton Free Public Library. Accessed February 2012.

Kehilla Links, http://kehilalinks.jewishgen.org/lida-district/wages.htm. October 14, 2013.

Korn, Bertram W, American Jewry and the Civil War (Philadelphia, PA: Jewish Publication Society of America, 1st 1951; 2d. ed., 1970).

Gay, Ruth (1984). "Inventing the Shtetl". The American Scholar 53 (3): 329–349.

Ginsburg, R. (2002, February 18). Remarks in appreciation. Paper presented at the annual presentation of the Jewish Council for Public Affairs, Albert D. Chemin Award meeting, New York.

Greene, Daniel, Reuben Cohen Comes of Age: American Jewish Youth and the Lived Experience of Cultural Pluralism in the 1920s. American Jewish History, Volume 95, Number 2, (June 2009).

Gottlieb, Andrew, Between Gemeinschaft and Gesselschaft: Jewish-American identity from the 1880s to the 1980s. Dissertation, (Union Institute & University, Cincinnati, 2009).

Dr. Gilbert Gold, Interview, February 2012; http://udini.proquest.com/view/between-gemeinschaft-and-goid:744300335

Sidney Goldmann's Papers on Early Trenton Jewry, Trenton Free Public Library. Accessed February 2012.

Sidney Goldmann's Papers for the Jewish Family Service, 1975.

Sidney Goldmann Dies at 79 - Jersey Administrative Judge... www.nytimes.com/.../sidney-goldmann-dies-at-79-j...Acc. September 15, 2015.

Gross, Max, Interview. May 3, 2012.

Hebrew Sheltering and Immigrant Aid Society, http://www.hias.org/ . Accessed May 11, 2012.

Hadassah, http://www.jewishmag.com/154mag/immigrant_pioneers/immigrant_pioneers.htm.

Harcave, Sidney, Years of the Golden Cockerel: The Last Romanov Tsars, 1814-1917 (NY: Macmillan Publishers, 1968).

History of New Jersey, from its earliest settlement to the present time. (Philadelphia, John E. Potter and Company, 1877) 2 v.

History of the city of Trenton, New Jersey. (Trenton, W. T. Nicholson & Co., 1871).

Hyman, Paula E., Eastern European Immigrants in the United States, http://jwa.org/encyclopedia/article/eastern-european-immigrants-in-united-states. Accessed July 8, 2013.

Hadassah, Trenton, NJ Minutes 1932-35. Trenton Free Library.

Hagen, William W., Germans, Poles, and Jews: The Nationality Conflict in the Prussian East, 1772- 1914 (Chicago: University of Chicago Press, 1980)

Har Sinai Temple, Trenton, http://www.jewishvirtuallibrary.org/jsource/judaica/ejud_0002_0020_0_20026.html. Accessed April 29

Hess, Jon A., Assimilating newcomers into an organization: A cultural perspective, Volume 21, Issue 2, 1993. www.tandfonline.com, Accessed May 30, 3014.

Heston, A. M., Jersey Wagon Jaunts; New Stories of New Jersey. Camden, Atlantic County, NJ Historical Society, 1926), 2 v.

Heston, A. M., South Jersey, A History, 1664-1924.(New York, Lewis Historical Publishing Co., 1924.), 5 v.

HIAS - Welcome the stranger. Protect the refugee. www.hias.org/. Accessed June 14, 2015.

History of Trenton, New Jersey (Trenton, F. T. Smiley & Co., 1895).

History of Trenton 1679-1929, (freepages.history.rootsweb.ancestry.com/~trenton/historyoftrenton/industries.htm)

The Trenton City Museum at Ellerslie, Accessed March 22, 2014. Beginning of an Industrial Giant, http://www.ellarslie.org/about_pottery.htm. 03/26/08; www.state.nj.us/counties/mercer/about/history/industrial-giant.html,

A History of Trenton 1679-1929, Accessed September 3, 2014.
(freepages.history.rootsweb.ancestry.com/~trenton/historyoftrenton/industries.ht
m.

The Immigrant Jews in America, Ed. Edmund J. James, (NY: Buck Co, 1907).

Kaufman, Rhoda Helfman, The Yiddish Theater In New York And The
Immigrant Jewish Community: Theater As Secular Ritual (Dissertation),
(Berkerly, CA: University of California, Berkeley, 1986).

The Kiev Jewish Emigration Society, http://www.rtrfoundation.org/kiev-1.html.
Accessed February 13, 2013.

Kriwaczek, Paul, Yiddish Civilisation: The Rise and Fall of a Forgotten
Nation (NY: Vintage Books, 2005.

The Jewish encyclopedia : a descriptive record of the history, religion, literature,
and customs of the Jewish people from the earliest times to the present day,
Singer, Isidore and Cyrus Adler, ed. (NY: KTAV Pubilsihing, c1910.
Ddigitilaixed   2008.   https://archive.org/details/jewishencycloped05sing.
Accessed November 2, 2013.

Joseph, Samuel, Jewish Immigration to the United States from 1881 to 1910:
Studies in History, Economics and Public Law, (Vol. LIX, No. 4, 1914). The
Project Gutenberg eBook, Release Date: February 27, 2011 [eBook #35415]

Jews, As Merchants, Making Great Progress in Trenton, Trenton Evening Times
(Trenton, NJ), March 9, 1913, p. 12

Jewish Virtual Library.
http://www.jewishvirtuallibrary.org/jsource/judaica/ejud_0002_0020_0_20026.
html, Accessed   January, 6, 2011

Jews in Trenton History, .Community Messenger. (September 1925).

Jewish Reformer and Intellectual (1994), and Lance Sussman, Isaac Leeser and
the Making of American Judaism (Detroit: Wayne State University Press, 1995).

Johnson, Elma Lawson, A History of Trenton 1679-1929, Trenton Historical
Society, http://trentonhistory.org/His/Social.html. Accessed June 15, 2012.

Kauffman, Benjamin. Benjamin Kaufman | Jewish Virtual Library
https://www.jewishvirtuallibrary.org/.../kaufman.ht....Accessed September 30,
2015.

KehilaLinks, http://kehilalinks.jewishgen.org/balta/hist.asp. Accessed November 10, 2013.

The Kiev Jewish Emigration Society, http://www.rtrfoundation.org/kiev-1.html. Accessed May 11, 2012.

Koch, Ashley L, Jewish Immigrant Communities in Ohio: A Microcosm of Early 20th Century America (Unpublished Thesis; Wash. D.C.: Georgetown U.; 2011).

Klier, John Doyle, Russia Gathers Her Jews: The Origins of the "Jewish Question" in Russia, 1772-1825 (DeKalb: Northern Illinois University Press, 1986.

Kohn, S.J., David Naar of Trenton, (New Jersey, Marstin Press, Inc.), www.jewishgen.org/jhscj/genealogy.html. Accessed December 13, 2013.

Koslow, Harold, Interview, April 9, 2012

Kriwaczek, Paul, Yiddish Civilization: The Rise and Fall of a Forgotten Nation (NY: Vintage Books, 2005).

Lavine, Mrs. Barry and A. Arthur Sugerman
http://www.iajgsjewishcemeteryproject.org/new-jersey/trenton-mercer-county.html. Accessed May 3, 2013.

Leeson, Dan, Military Conscription in Russia in the 19th Century, http://www.jewishgen.org/ infofiles/ru-mil.txt. Accessed September 5, 2013.

Lilienthal, Max American Zionist Journal (NY: 1846), p. 449; 1847, p.21 ff.

Litowitz, Mark (Hon.), Interview, November 21, 2011.

Lodz, Textiles and Industry, http://www.textilehistory.org/NewJersey.html. Accessed October 6, 2012.

Lodz, http://epyc.yivo.org/content/17_4.php. Accessed October 6,, 2012.

Mintz, Sidney W., and Christine M. Du Bois, The Anthropology of Food and Eating, Annual Review of Anthropology, (Vol. 31, 2002), pp. 99-119.

Langston, Scott Langston, Interaction and Identity: Jews and Christians in Nineteenth Century New Orleans, Southern Jersey Jewish Historical Society. (Scott Langston, Interaction and Identity: Jews and Christians in Nineteenth Century New Orleans, Southern Jersey Jewish Historical Society (Vol. 3, 2000)

Laskin, Janet, Interview, April 30, 2012.

Law on Taxes, Secs. 1, 5, 8, to Sec. 281, Vol. V., 1857.

Lavine, Mrs. Barry, and A. Arthur Sugerman, 15 February 2001, http://www.iajgsjewishcemeteryproject.org/new-jersey/trenton-mercer-county.html. Accessed March 5, 2012.

Lee, Francis Bazley, History of Trenton, Trenton, State Gazette, 1985.

Lederhendler, Eli, Jewish Immigration and American Capitalism, 1800-1920, (Cambridge: Cambridge University Press, 2009).

Francis Lee, New Jersey as a Colony and as a State, Occident, Vol. 24, p 40, 1902.

Lippy, C., Faith in America: Changes, challenges, and new directions. (Santa Barbara, CA: Greenwood, 2006).

Luxemburg, Rosa, The Mass Strike, the Political Party and the Trade Unions (NY: Harper Torchbooks, originally published, 1906).

Mahler, Raphael, "The Economic Background of Jewish Emigration from Galicia to the United States," in East European Jews in Two Worlds: Studies from the YIVO Annual, ed. Deborah Dash Moore (Evanston, Ill.: YIVO and Northwestern University Press, 1990) pp. 125-137.

Marcus, Jacob Rader, The Colonial American Jew (Philadelphia, PA: Jewish Publication Society, 1970).

Mandel, Irving Aaron, Attitude of the American Jewish Community toward East-European Immigration As Reflected In The Anglo-Jewish Press (1880-1890). Diss. (NY: 1947).

Markens, The Hebrews in America (New York, 1888) pp. 231–232.

McClure, Archibald, Leadership for the New America (Chicago: George H. Doran Co., 1916).

McCulloch John, The Bridge (NY: Simon and Shuster, Inc., 1972).

McGowan, Brother Denis P., who provided the history of these Orders. Brother Denis P. McGowan is a dedicated fraternalist and student of the history of American fraternal organizations (NY: City Record), Vol 33, Part 5.

Mercer County, Beginning of Industrial Giant, Accessed May 11, 2012: http://www.state.nj.us/counties/mercer/about/history/industrial-giant.html.

Mercer Messenger, ed. Sidney Goldman, (Trenton, NJ, YMHA, 1925-1932).

Merzbacher John S., Trenton's Foreign Colonies A description of the homes, habits, customs, languages, attributes and activities of the non-English speaking residents of Trenton, Trenton Sunday Advertiser, December 5, 1908.

Meyer, Michael A. "German-Jewish Identity in Nineteenth-Century America," in Jacob Katz (ed.), Toward Modernity: The European Jewish Model (New Brunswick. N.J., 1987) pp. 247-67.

Meyer, Michael A. Response to Modernity: A History of the Reform Movement in Judaism, Studies in Jewish History. New York: Oxford University Press 1988)

Mintz, Steven, Housework in Late 19th Century America. http://www.digitalhistory.uh.edu/historyonline/housework.cfm. Accessed May 2, 2014.

Morais, Lloyd P. Gartner, Nezhin in Philadelphia: The Families and Occupations of an Immigrant Congregation, Jewish History, Vol. 8, No. 1/2, The Robert Cohen Memorial Volume (1994), pp. 229-253. Stable URL: http://www.jstor.org/stable/20101199. Accessed 14/05/2012 14:08.

Morawska, Ewa, American Jewish History, (Volume 88, Number 4, December 2000). Accessed November 14, 2013.

A Microcosm of Early 20th Century America, Unpublished Thesis, Georgetown University, Washington, D.C. ProQuest, UMI Dissertation Publishing (September 2, 2011).

Naar, Devin, Tracing the Origins of the Naars of New Jersey: A Personal Odyssey, http://www.jewishgen.org/jhscj/genealogy.html. Acc. March 15, 2012.

National Humanities Center, http://nationalhumanitiescenter.org/tserve/nineteen. Accessed September 3, 2013.

Ornea, Z., Anii treizeci. Extrema dreaptă românească[("The 1930s: The Romanian Far Right"], Bucharest. Romania: Editura Fundaţiei Culturale România, 1995).

Olegario, Rowena, a Culture of Credit (Cambridge, MA: President and Scholars of Harvard College, 2006).

Olegario,Rowena, "That Mysterious People": Jewish Merchants, Transparency, and Community in Mid-Nineteenth Century America, Harvard College, The Business History Review, Vol. 73, No. 2 (Summer, 1999), pp. 161-189.Stable URL: http://www.jstor.org/stable/3116239. Accessed11/05/2012 15:28.

Olmstead, Frederick LW, Our Parks, http://www.olmstedparks.org/our-parks/. Accessed April 15, 2013.

The Pale of Settlement - Jewish Virtual Library, www.jewishvirtuallibrary.org/jsource/History/pale.html. Accessed March 15, 2012.

Penkower, Monty Noam The Kishinev Pogrom of 1903: A Turning Point in Jewish History, Modern Judaism. Vol. 24, No. 3. (Oct. 2004). pp. 187-225.

Pettysrun Archeological Excavations, http://www.pettysrun.org/. Acc. May 29, 2012.

Pinchuk, Ben Cion, Shtetls, http://www.tachna.com/stetls.html. Acc. March 15, 2012.

Piaget, Jean, Accommodation and Assimilation. http://ute.umh.ac.be/dutice/uv6a/ Accessed April 5, 2014. http://www.learningandteaching.info/learning/piaget.htm.

Pale of the Settlement, Jewish Virtual Kibrary. Accessed May 1, 2014, http://www.jewishvirtuallibrary.org/jsource/History/pale.html.

Perlman, R. , From Shtetl to Milltown: Litvaks, Hungarians, and Galizianers in Western Pennsylvania, 1875–1925 (Pittsburgh, 2001).

Plaut, W. Gunther, The Rise of Reform Judaism, (NY: World Union for Progressive Judaism, 1963).

Philipson, David. The Reform Movement in Judaism. A reissue of the new and revised with an introduction by Solomon B. Freehof, 3rd. ed. (London, New York, Macmillan, 1907).

Plaut, W. Gunther. The Rise of Reform Judaism: A Sourcebook of Its European Origins. (New York: World Union of Progressive Judaism, 1963).

Podmore, Harry J., Trenton, Old and New. Trenton, Kenneth W. Moore Company, 1927. May 5, 1013.

Podmore, Harry J., Trenton Historical Society, http://www.trentonhistory.org/1929history.html, Accessed May 11, 2012.

Podmore, Harry J, Trenton Historical Society, Accessed May 11, 2012: http://www.trentonhistory.org/Buildings/EndangeredSites2011.pdf.

Podmore, Harry J, Churches and Religious Institutions, (Trenton, NJ: Trenton Historical Society, 1929).

Podmore, Harry J., Trenton Times-Advertiser, Sunday Times-Advertiser, October 24, 1943.

Podmore, H. J., "The head of town," and other articles on early Trenton. Scrapbook of newspaper clippings in Trenton Free Public Library.

Potteries of Trenton Society, http://www.potteriesoftrentonsociety.org/, Accessed May 10, 2012. Accessed May 11, 2012.

Raison, Jacob, Haskala Movement in Russia (Philadelphia: The Jewish Publication Society of America, 1913).

Raison,Max A., A History of The Jews In Modern Times (NY: Hebrew Pub. Co. in New York, 1919).

Raum, J. O. History Of The City Of Trenton, New Jersey: Embracing A Period Of Nearly Two Hundred Years, Commencing In 1676…, 1871 (W.T. Nicholson & Company, printers, 1871).

Rawidowicz, S. (1998). Israel: The ever-dying people. In S. Rawidowicz (Ed.), State of Israel, diaspora, and Jewish continuity, Rev. ed. (Lebanon, NH: Brandeis University Press, 1998) pp. 53-58.

Joseph Rice Dies at Belmar Home, Trenton Evening Times, July 15, 1913.

Riis, Jacob, Battle with the Slum (London: The Macmillan Company, Ltd., 1902).

Diana Riker's Research Blog, http://driker.wordpress.com/tag/trenton/. Nov. 8, 2012.

Rosenthal, Herman, Romania and the Jews, The North American Review, (Vol. 186, No. 624, Nov., 1907), pp. 400-404.
Stable URL: http://www.jstor.org/stable/25106026. Accessed 14/05/2012 16:24

Rubin, Debra, Ahavath Israel, in midst of a merger, marks its centennial A bittersweet celebration, New Jersey Jewish News, April 12, 2010;
http://njjewishnews.com/article/1127/a-bittersweet-celebration#.UPnA3GeoR8E. Accessed June 15, 2012.

Rubin, Lloyd, How to Bring Back Grandma's Yiddish Cooking,), The Jewish Magazine. (December, 2005)
www.jewishmag.com/97mag/grandmacooking/grandmacooking.htm. Accessed May 13, 2013.

Robinson S., Jewish Population of Trenton, N.J. (NY: Conference of Jewish Relations, 1949).

Rosenberg, Elliot, But Were They Good for the Jews? Over 150 Historical Figures Viewed from a Jewish Perspective) Secaucus, NJ: Carol Pub. Group, 1997).

Rosenstein, Rosenberg Neil, The Grandees of New Jersey: Naar, Baiz, Peixotto, Pretto & Seixas Families (Elizabeth, NJ: Computer Center for Jewish Genealogy, 2006).

Rothenberg, Joshua, Demythologizing the Shtetl, Midstream (March 1981): 25-31.

Russia - Transformation of Russia in the Nineteenth Century countrystudies.us/russia/6.htm. Accessed September 15, 2015.

Sachar, Howard Morley. The Course of Modern Jewish History. New rev. ed. (New York: Vintage Books, 1990).

Samuel, Henry, Jews of Philadelphia, (Philadelphia, The Levytype Co., 1894)

Santrock, John WA topical approach to life-span development, 4th ed. (New York City: McGraw-Hill, 2008).

Sarna, Jonathan D, American Judaism: A History (New Haven, CT:Yale University Press, 2004).

Sarna, Jonathan, The American Jewish Experience, 2nd Edition, ed. (Teaneck, NJ: Holmes & Meier Publishers 1986, 1997).

Sarna, Jonathan, ed. by Marshall Sklare. Observing America's Jews. Brandeis University Press/UPNE, 1993).

Sarna, Jonathan, American Judaism: A History (New Haven, CT: Yale University Press, 2004).

Sarna, Jonathan, "Jewish Culture Comes to America." Jewish Studies (Vol. 42, (2003): 45-57.

Sarna, Jonathan and Jonathan Golden The American Jewish Experience through the Nineteenth Century: Immigration and Acculturation,

http://nationalhumanitiescenter.org/tserve/nineteen/nkeyinfo/judaism.htm. Accessed   April 13, 2013.

Scenes from a Luncheonette-Remembering Greenfield's (May 10, 2011). http://trentonjewishproject.blogspot.com/2011/05/scenes-from-luncheonette-remembering.html. Accessed May 1, 2014.

Sclar. Arieh, "A Sport at which Jews Excel": Jewish Basketball in American Society, 1900—1951, (Stoney Brook, NY: State University of New York at Stony Brook, 2009)

Schappes, Morris U. A Documentary History of the Jews in the United States, 1654-1875 (NY: Schocken Press, 3rd ed., 1971).

Segal, Alex - IMDb. www.imdb.com/name/nm0781751/. Acc. Sept. 15, 2015.

Seltzer, Robert M. Jewish People, Jewish Thought: The Jewish Experience in History. (New York: Macmillan, 1980.

Shelly v. Kramer, 334 U.S. 1 (1948).

Siegel, Seymour, and Elliot Gertel. God in the Teachings of Conservative Judaism, Emet Ve*Emunah; V. 3 (New York, Hoboken: N.J.: Rabbinical Assembly ; Distributed by KTAV, 1985).

Siegle, Tony - San Francisco Giants;
sanfrancisco.giants.mlb.com/sf/.../siegle_tony.jsp. Accessed September 30, 2015.

Steiner, Edward A. The Immigrant Tide: It's Ebb And Flow (NY: Fleming V. Revell, 1910).

Stern, Marc Jeffrey, The Pottery Industry of Trenton (New Brunswick, NJ: Rutgers University. Press, 1994).

Schenectady County Historical Society,
http://schenectadyhist.wordpress.com/page/2/. Accessed May 9, 2012.

Schenectady, NY, http://schenectadyhist.wordpress.com/page/2/. Accessed May 9, 2012.

Schenectady, NY, http://schenectadyhist.wordpress.com/page/2/. Accessed May September 4, 2012

Sherman, C. Bezalel, "The Jews within American Society" (Detroit, Wayne State University Press, 1961)

Shtetl - Jewish Virtual Library, Accessed December 15, 2015,
www.jewishvirtuallibrary.org/jsource/judaica/ejud_0002_0018_0

Shulman, Matt, Trenton's 'Jewtown' lives again — on the web, New Jersey Jewish News, (January 13, 2012).
http://njjewishnews.com/article/7928/trentons-jewtown-lives-again-on-the-web#.U2Ly4_ldV8G. Accessed May 1, 2014.

Siegel, Alex. www.gutenberg.org/files/17385/17385-r.rtf. Accessed January 28, 2016.

Tony Siegle - San Francisco Giants: Front Office. sanfrancisco.giants.mlb.com/sf/team/frontoffice_bios/siegle_tony.jsp. Accessed January 28, 2016.

Silverstein, Len, Interview November 18, 2012.

Stern, Marc Jeffrey, The Pottery Industry of Trenton: A Skilled Trade in Transition, 1850-1929, The Journal of American History, Vol. 82, No. 2 (Sep., 1995), p. 736; Organization of American Historians Stable, http://www.jstor.org/stable/2082274 .Accessed   : 11/04/2012 07:20 pm.

Spector, Scott, Forget Assimilation: Introducing Subjectivity to German-Jewish History, Jewish History, (NY: Springer. Publisher, 2006), Vol. 20, No. 3/4, pp. 349-361. http://www.jstor.org/stable/2010. Accessed 11/05/2012 15:20.

Scott Spector, Forget Assimilation: Introducing Subjectivity to German-Jewish History, Jewish History, Vol. 20, No. 3/4 (2006), pp. 349-361. Published by: Springer. URL: http://www.jstor.org/stable/2010. Accessed: 11/05/2012 15:20

Skierniewice, Jewish Virtual Library. http://www.jewishvirtuallibrary.org/jsource/judaica/ejud_0002_0018_0_18416. html. Accessed February 13, 2013.

Springfield/Belmont, Newark, New Jersey, http://en.wikipedia.org/wiki/Springfield/Belmont,_Newark,_New_Jersey.   June 5, 2013.

Stark, Albert Interview, reciting notes form Emil Stark on Crothers of Israel synagogue. February 2012.

Timeline based on information from www.nps.gov/upde/roebaque.html. Accessed April 5, 2014.

Teicher, Rabbi Paul, The Jewish Organizations Incorporated In Mercer County New Jersey 1857—1964, consulting Their Incorporators (Farmingdale New York, Farmingdale Jewish Center, 1967. Source from Incorporations, Religious Societies, Volumes A - C. (Vol. C was current in 1964); Merzbacher, John S., Trenton's Foreign Colonies. Trenton: Press of Beers & Frey, 1908; Paul Teicher, "The Dr. Herzl Zion Hebrew School, a History, 1883-1964," appearing in the

School's Scholarship Dinner Journal, January 31, 1964, Trenton, N. J.; and interviews with Mr. Leon Kasman, in 1966.

Trenton Historical Society, History of Trenton 1679 – 1929, (Trenton, NJ: Trenton Historical Commission, 1929); J.S. Merzbacher, Trenton's Foreign Colonies (Trenton, NJ: Beers and Frey,1908); Kohn, in: AJHSQ, (1964), Vol/. 53, 373–95.

The Trenton City Museum at Ellerslie, Accessed September 3, 2014: http://www.ellarslie.org/about_pottery.htm. Updated 03/26/08.

Trenton Times-Advertiser

Trenton Transit, Terminal Cab Company, Employee Yearly Earnings Records, 1937-45. Trenton Free Public Library.

Trenton State Gazette.

Trenton True American.

Virtual Jewish World: New Jersey, United States, Accessed October 8, 2012: http://www.jewishvirtuallibrary.org/jsource/judaica/ejud_0002_0015_0_14777.html.

Virtual Jewish Virtual Library, Accessed January 6, 2013. http://www.jewishvirtuallibrary.org/jsource/judaica/ejud_0002_,

Voices from a Paterson Silk Mill - Bergen Academy and... sites.bergen.org/ourstory/Resources/.../Voices_from_silk_mill.pdf.   Accessed September 15, 2014.

Waldinger, Roger, Through the Eye of the Needle: Immigrants and Enterprise in New York's Garment Trades (New York University Press, 1986; paper, 1989).

Weber Commission Report, (Washington, DC: Congressional Printing Office, 1894).

Weinberg, Robert. The Revolution of 1905 in Odessa: Blood on the Steps. (Indianapolis, IN: Indiana University Press 1993) p. 164.

Weinfeld Morton, The Encyclopedia of Canada's Peoples/, Jews/, http://www.multiculturalcanada.ca/Encyclopedia/A-Z/j3/1F. Accessed June 4, 2013.

Weingarten, Irving, The Image Of The Jew In The American Periodical Press, 1881-1921. (NY: New York University, 1980, Unpub Dissertation).

Weiner, Deborah R. The Jews of Keystone: Life in a Multicultural Boomtown, (Vineland, NJ: Southern Jersey Jewish Historical Society, 1999).

Weinryb, Bernard D., East European Immigration to the United States, The Jewish Quarterly Review, (New Series, Vol. 45, No. 4, Tercentenary Issue, April,

1955), pp. 497-528. Stable URL: http://www.jstor.org/stable/1452943, Accessed 07/06/2012.

Sol Weinstein, A Personal Lament, Trentonian 6/24/1926.

Weiss, J. R. (2000). The Metamorphosis of Jewish Identities In Nineteenth Century Russia, 1801--1894. (Wheeling, WV: West Virginia University, ProQuest Dissertations and Theses), 420.

Werthheimer, J., The American Synagogue: A Sanctuary Transformed. (Cambridge: Cambridge University Press, 2003).

http://search.proquest.com/docview/304634534?accountid=11809. Accessed May26, 2013.

Walcoff, Victor Esq., e-mail, dated February 24, 2013.

Weber Commission on Immigration (Washington. DC: GPO, 1893).

YIVO Institute,
 http://www.yivoinstitute.org/digital_exhibitions/index.php?mcid=69&oid=10. Accessed   November 11, 2013.

Young Judaea, Accessed September 4, 2012:
http://www.youngjudaea.org/site/c.nuIYKfMWIvF/b.6091445/k.C539/History.htm.

Zeltmacher, Meriel, Interview, April 30, 2012.

Zollman, Joellyn Shtetl in Jewish History and Memory: Of flying fiddlers & the gefilte fish line.
http://www.myjewishlearning.com/history/Modern_History/1700-1914/traditional-jewish-life/Shtetls.shtml. Accessed June 14, 2013.

Zosa Szajkowski, Sufferings of Jewish Emigrants to America in Transit through Germany, Jewish Social Studies, (Winter - Spring, 1977), pp. 105-116, Vol. 39, No. 1/2, American Bicentennial: II http://www.jstor.org/stable/4466952. Accessed 12/06/2013 14:38

Ozzie Zuckerman's Papers on Early Trenton Jewry, Trenton Free Public Library. Accessed February 2012.

ENDNOTES

[1] John McCulloch, The Bridge (NY: Simon and Shuster, Inc., 1972)

[2] http://driker.wordpress.com/tag/trenton/. Accessed January 12, 2010.

[3] http://driker.wordpress.com/tag/trenton/. Accessed January 12, 2010.

[4] http://driker.wordpress.com/tag/trenton/. Accessed January 12, 2010.

[5] Journal of the Proceedings of the Convention to form a Constitution (Trenton, 1844), pp. 12, 30, 43 ff., 269 ff; and 292; PAJHS, vol. XVII (1909), p. 41.

[6] Rabbi S. Joshua Kohn, David Naar of Trenton, New Jersey Kohn, S Joshua American Jewish Historical Quarterly, (June 1, 1964) pp 53, 4; Periodicals Archive Online pg. 373. Accessed April 24, 2014.

[7] Rabbi S. Joshua Kohn, David Naar of Trenton, New Jersey Kohn, S Joshua American Jewish Historical Quarterly, (June 1, 1964) pp 53, 4; Periodicals Archive Online pg. 373. Accessed April 24, 2014.

[8] Rabbi S. Joshua Kohn, David Naar of Trenton, New Jersey Kohn, S Joshua American Jewish Historical Quarterly, (June 1, 1964) pp 53, 4; Periodicals Archive Online pg. 373. Acc. April 24, 2014

[9] Rabbi S. Joshua Kohn, David Naar of Trenton, New Jersey Kohn, S Joshua American Jewish Historical Quarterly, (June 1, 1964) pp 53, 4; Periodicals Archive Online pg. 373. Acc. April 24, 2014; A family's lost story found, and the Sephardic Studies ... www.washington.edu/news/.../16/...and-the-sephardic-studies-initiative Jan 16, 2013. Devin Narr traced his family from Portugal to Amsterdam. Then it split into three: Salonika, Greece, London and the Dutch West Indies.

[10] Harry J. Podmore, Trenton – Old and New, Trenton Historical society, (Trenton: Kenneth W. Moore Company, 1927).Accessed   June15, 2012

[11] Judiaca, http://www.jewishvirtuallibrary.org/jsource/judaica/ejud_0002_. Accessed Feb. 10, 2013.

[12] Sidney Goldmann's Papers on Early Trenton Jewry, Trenton Free Public Library. Ac. Feb. 2012.

[13] Trenton Evening Times, of July 15, 1913.

[14] S. Ettinger, "Serkele" and "Der Fetter in America," reprinted in S. Ettinger,ed. (M. Weinreich, Wilno, 1925).

[15] Jews, As Merchants, Making Great Progress In Trenton, (Trenton, NJ: Trenton Evening Times, March 9, 1913), p. 12

[16] History of Trenton, Trenton Historical Society, 1929, http://freepages.history.rootsweb.ancestry.com/~trenton/historyoftrenton/church es/jews.htm. Accessed August 21, 2014.

[17] The Hebrews in South Trenton a Large and Prosperous Colony: Isaac Goodstein Was the Pioneer, Trenton Evening Times; April 13, 1902.

[18] Albert Stark (Grandson), Interview, March 22, 2012.

[19] Trenton In Bygone Days, Sunday Trenton Evening Times (Trenton, NJ, Oct. 24, 1943), p

[20] H. S. Linfield, Ph. D., Statistics of Jews, American Jewish Year Book (NY: American Jewish Committee, 1923).

[21] Harry J. Podmore, Trenton – Old and New, Trenton Historical society, 1929, 1903 Trenton Ordinance.

[22] Trenton's Jewish Community: The Second Generation. http://trentonjewishhistoricalsociety.blogspot.com/p/trentons-jewtown.html. Acc. August 22, 2014.

[23] Harry Gerofsky papers, Collections at Trenton Free Library, Trentoniana, January 2012.

[24] Koch, Ashley L, .Jewish Immigrant Communities in Ohio: A Microcosm of Early 20th Century America (Unpublished Thesis; Wash. D.C.: Georgetown U.; 2011).

[25] American Jewish Year Book,, 1915 (*NY: American Jewish Committee, 1915)

[26] Michael Kuzma, former resident of Fall Street, January 2013.

[27] Matt Schuman. "Jewtown Lives Again On The Web, New Jersey News, January 13, 2012. http://njjewishnews.com/article/7928/trentons-jewtown-lives-again-on-the-web#.T0BFSPEgdOt. Accessed August 22, 2014.

[28] Scenes From Luncheonette,http://trentonjewishproject.blogspot.com/2011/05/scenes-from-luncheonette-remembering.html. Accessed August 22, 2014.

[29] See Appendix 4.

[30] See Mercer Messenger, 1925-1931.

[31] Trenton Times, 1904, genealogybank.com. Accessed February 12, 2012.

[32] Harry J. Podmore's news articles of the dedication appeared in the Community Messenger and Trenton Evening Times, 1928.

33 Appendix 3

[34] Har Sinai articles, Trenton Times, 1904 to 1969.

[35] Harry Podmore, Trenton Historical Society (Trenton, 1929).

[36] Gold, Dr. Gilbert, Interview.2012-March 2014.)His father was a founding member of the synagogue and a manager of the cigar factory.)

[37] A Bittersweet Celebration, http://njjewishnews.com/article/1127/a-bittersweet-celebration#.UPnA3GeoR8E. Accessed August 22, 2014.

[38] John S. Merzbacher, Trenton's Foreign Colonies A description of the homes, habits, customs, languages, attributes and activities of the non-English speaking residents of Trenton, Trenton Sunday Advertiser, December 5, 1908.

[39] Oct 1926 Podmore, Jewish Messenger; Ozzie Zuckerman NJN 12/19/99.

[40] http://trentonhistory.org/His/Social.html. Accessed January 25, 2012.

[41] See Evening Times, Thursday, October 10, 1901.

[42] See Trenton Evening Times, January 7, 1901.

[43] See Banquet And Cards For Ladies At Progress Club, Trenton Evening Times, Nov 28 1913.

[44] See Evening Times, May 6, 1914.

[45] Sale of Handsome Broughton Home To Progress Club Has Been Consummated; Auditorium Will Be Added, Trenton Evening Times (Trenton, NJ), Sunday, April 30, 1922.

[46] Interview with Victor Walcoff, Esq., March 2013.

[47] Tony Fels "Religious Assimilation in the Fraternal Organization: Jews and Freemasonry in Gilded-Age San Francisco." 74 American Jewish History (June 1985).

[48] Tony Fels "Religious Assimilation in the Fraternal Organization: Jews and Freemasonry in Gilded-Age San Francisco." 74 American Jewish History (June 1985

[49] Podmore, supra.

[50] Sclar. Arieh, "A Sport at which Jews Excel": Jewish Basketball in American Society, 1900—1951, (Stoney Brook, NY: State University of New York at Stony Brook, 2009).

51 Trenton Evening Times, January 10 , 1934.

52 Bloom, Meyer, http://www.jewsinsports.org/profile.asp?sport=basketball&ID=106. Accessed April 17, 2014.

53 Ben Olinsky, http://trentonjewishproject.blogspot.com/2011/11/memory-of-ben-olinsky.html. Accessed December 5, 2011

54 Brody, Tal, http://www.tutorgig.info/ed/Tal_Brody. Accessed April 11, 2014.

55 (The Yiddish Theater in New York and The Immigrant Jewish Community: Theater as Secular Ritual, Diss. Kaufman, Rhoda Helfman. University of California, Berkeley, 1986. 1986. 8718038).

56 Harry Gerofsky's Papers on Early Trenton Jewry, Trenton Free Public Library. Acc. Feb. 2012.

57 Podmore, HarryJ,Churches and Religious Institutions, (Trenton , NJ: Trenton Historical Society, 1929).

58 Podmore, supra.

59 Litowitz, Mark (Hon.), Interview, November 21, 2011.

60 Harry Podmore, Trenton True Gazette Story, 1913

61 *Har Sinai Temple*, Trenton
http://www.jewishvirtuallibrary.org/jsource/judaica/ejud_0002_0020_0_20026.html Accessed April 29, 2014.

60 Andrew Gottlieb, Between Gemeinschaft and Gesselschaft: Jewish-American identity from the 1880s to the 1980s. Dissertation (Union Institute & University, Cincinnati, 2009).

63 Jon A. Hess Assimilating newcomers into an organization: A cultural perspective, Volume 21, Issue 2, 1993. www.tandfonline.com, Accessed   May 30, 3014.

64 http://www.bls.gov/opub/uscs/1934-36.pdf. Accessed January 15, 2013.

65 Schenectady County Historical Society, http://schenectadyhist.wordpress.com/page/2/. Accessed May 9, 2012; Schenectady, NY, http://schenectadyhist.wordpress.com/page/2/. Accessed May 9, 2012; Schenectady, NY, http://schenectadyhist.wordpress.com/page/2/. Accessed May September 4, 2012

66 Olmstead, Frederick LW, Our Parks, http://www.olmstedparks.org/our-parks/. Accessed April 15, 2013.

67 Cadwalader Park Master Plan, http://www.trentonnj.org/PARKS/CWP_Plan_Chapter3.html Accessed April 15, 2013.

68 Cadwalader Park, http://www.trentonnj.org/PARKS/CadwaladerPark.html. Accessed April 15, 2013.

69 Voices from a Paterson Silk Mill - Bergen Academy and ...
sites.bergen.org/ourstory/Resources/.../Voices_from_silk_mill.pdf. Accessed September 15, 2014.

70 John T. Cumbler, Social History of Economic Decline: Business, Politics, and Work in Trenton (New Brunswick: Rutgers Press. 1989)

71 Supra.

72 Supra.

73 Supra.

[74] Eugene I. Bender and George Kagiwada, Hansen's Law of "Third-Generation Return" and the Study of American Religio-Ethnic Groups, Phylon (Clark Atlanta University, 1960-2002), Vol. 29, No. 4 (4th Qtr., 1968), pp. 360-370. :http://www.jstor.org/stable/274020.

[75] Sidney Goldmann Dies at 79 - Jersey Administrative Judge ... www.nytimes.com/.../sidney-goldmann-dies-at-79-j...Accessed September 15, 2015.

[76] Kauffman, Benjamin. Benjamin Kaufman | Jewish Virtual Library https://www.jewishvirtuallibrary.org/.../kaufman.ht....Accessed September 30, 2015.

[77] Matthew Dallas, Curtain falls on Plimmerton schmoozer, Obituary, Kapi-Mana News, New Zealand.

http://www.stuff.co.nz/dominion-post/news/local-papers/kapi-mana-news/8031003/Curtain-falls-on-Plimmerton-schmoozer. Accessed August 23, 2014; Remembering Sol Weinstein, a local comic genius, Variety Magazine,http://variety.com/2012/scene/news/tv-comedy-writer-sol-weinstein-dies-1118063040/ DECEMBER 3, 2012, Accessed August 23, 2014

[78] Alex Segal - IMDb. www.imdb.com/name/nm0781751/. Accessed September 15, 2009.

[79] Sol Linowtiz, http://www.washingtonpost.com/wp-dyn/articles/A47416-2005Mar18_4.html. Accessed August 24, 2014. Sol Myron Linowitz Biography http://www.biography.com/people/sol-myron-linowitz-9382881#the-diplomat. Acc. Aug. 24, 2014.

[80] "Big Think Interview with Judith Light". *BigThink.com*. May 10, 2010. Acc. Aug. 24, 2014. Judith Light - IMDb, www.imdb.com/name/nm0509937/. Accessed August 24, 2014.

[81] Douglas Martin, Zalman King, Creator of Soft-Core Films, Dies at 70 New York Times, February 8, 2012, http://www.nytimes.com/2012/02/09/arts/television/zalman-king-creator-of-soft-core-films-dies-at-70.html?_r=0. Accessed August 24, 2014; Zalman King. http://www.imdb.com/name/nm0455394/. Accessed August 24, 2014.

[82] Tony Siegle - San Francisco Giants; sanfrancisco.giants.mlb.com/sf/.../siegle_tony.jsp. Accessed September 30, 2015.

[83] Jonathan D. Sarna, American Judaism,: A History,(New Haven, CN, Yale University Press, 2004)

[84] Diner, Hasia, A Time for Gathering: The Second Migration, 1820-1880 (Baltimore, MD: Johns Hopkins Press, 1992).

[85] Stephen Birmingham, Our Crowd: The Great Jewish Families of New York, Syracuse, NY: First Syracuse University Press, 1996.

[86] Olegario, Rowena, a Culture Of Credit (Cambridge, MA: President and Scholars of Harvard College, 2006)

[87] Joseph Seligman, http://www.jewishencyclopedia.com/articles/13403-seligman. Accessed August 21, 2014.

[88] Morris-Schappe, Jewish Mass Immigration from Eastern Europe, 1881-1914. jewishcurrents.org/.../Jewish-Mass-Immigration-E-Europe-Morris-Schap... Accessed February 13, 2012

[89] Assimilation and Authenticity: The Problem of the American ... www.jcpa.org/dje/books/cp2-ch1.htm. Jerusalem Center for Public Affairs

[90] Jonathan Sarna. The American Jewish Experience, 2nd ed. (New York: Holmes and Meier, 1997).

[91] Kehilla Links, http://kehilalinks.jewishgen.org/lida-district/wages.htm. October 14, 2013.

[92] Perlman, R. , *From Shtetl to Milltown: Litvaks, Hungarians, and Galizianers in Western Pennsylvania, 1875–1925* (Pittsburgh, 2001).

[93] Russia - Transformation of Russia in the Nineteenth Century countrystudies.us/russia/6.htm. Accessed September 15, 2015.

[94] Dubnow, Simon,, History Of The Jews In Russia And Poland: From The Death Of Alexander I Until The Death Of Alexander III, Vol. II, (1825-1894). Philadelphia: The Jewish Publication Society Of America 1918. A Project Gutenberg EBook,

[95] Pogrom, http://dictionary.reference.com/browse/pogrom. Accessed February 13, 2013.

[96] Oscar Handlin, The Uprooted (Boston, 1952); Jewish Migration from the Russian Empire to the U.S. ... - EH.Net, eh.net/eha/wp-content/uploads/2013/11/Spitzer.pdf; Russian Jewish Immigration 1880-1920 - Fitchburg State University; www.fitchburgstate.edu/uploads/.../TeachingAmericanHistory/RussianJews. Accessed July 5, 2015

[97] American Jewish History americanjewiwshhistory.blogspot.com/. Accessed June 14, 2014.

[98] Pinchuk, Ben Cion, Shtetls, http://www.tachna.com/stetls.html. Accessed March 15, 2012

[99] Education - Jewish Virtual Library https://www.jewishvirtuallibrary.org/.../ejud_0002....Accessed September 30, 2015

[100] Education - Jewish Virtual Library. https://www.jewishvirtuallibrary.org/.../ejud_0002....Accessed September 30, 2015.

[101] Weber Commission Report, (Washington, DC: Congressional Printing Office, 1894). .org/jsource/judaica/ejud_0002

[102] Supra.

[103] Raison, Jacob,,Haskala Movement in Russia (Philadelphia: The Jewish Publication Society of America, 1913).

[104] Weber, supra, p. 152

[105] Weber, supra.

[106] Weber, supra.

[107] Weber, supra.

[108] Dubnow, Simon,, History Of The Jews In Russia And Poland: From The Death Of Alexander I Until The Death Of Alexander III, Vol. II, (1825-1894). Philadelphia: The Jewish Publication Society of America 1918. A Project Gutenberg EBook,

http://www.gutenberg.org/author/Simon_Dubnow.Accessed September 6, 2012.

[109] Jewish Pogroms - geni.com www.geni.com/projects/Jewish-Pogroms/24693.

[110] Joseph, Samuel, Jewish Immigration to the United States from 1881 to 1910: Studies in History, Economics and Public Law, (Vol. LIX, No. 4, 1914). The Project Gutenberg eBook, Release Date: February 27, 2011 [eBook #35415]

[111] Pogroms of Balta, http://www.jewishvirtuallibrary.org/jsource/History/pogroms.html.Accessed January 2, 2013.

[112] Modern History Sourcebook: The Treaty of Berlin, 1878. Excerpts on the Balkans, Treaty Between Great Britain, Austria-Hungary, France, Germany, Italy, Russia and Turkey. (Berlin). July 13, 1878. http://www.fordham.edu/halsall/mod/1878berlin.asp. Accessed August 22, 2013.

[113] Ornea, Z., The 1930s: The Romanian Far Right"], Bucharest. Romania: Editura Fundaţiei Culturale România,, 1995).

[114] Joseph, Samuel, Jewish Immigration to the United States from 1881 to 1910: Studies in History, Economics and Public Law, (Vol. LIX, No. 4, 1914). The Project Gutenberg eBook, Release Date: February 27, 2011 [eBook #35415]

[115] *Chy Lung v. Freeman* (92 U.S. 275, 1875).

[116] Edgardo Zablotsky, The Project of the Baron de Hirsch: Success or Failure? (University of CEMA, Buenos Aires, Arg., May 2005)

[117] The Galveston Movement - My Jewish Learning
www.myjewishlearning.com/.../the-galveston-movem...Accessed January 2, 2016.

[118] HIAS - Welcome the stranger. Protect the refugee.
www.hias.org/. Accessed June 14, 2015

[119] Mrs. Barry Lavine and A.S. Sugarman, 2001 International Jewish Cemetery Project (International Association of Jewish Genealogical Societies, 2001).
http://www.iajgsjewishcemeteryproject.org/new-jersey/trenton-mercer-county.html.
Accessed May 4, 2012.

[120] Rabbi Paul Teicher, The Jewish Organizations Incorporated In Mercer County New Jersey 1857—1964, consulting Their Incorporators (Farmingdale New York, Farmingdale Jewish Center, 1967. Source from Incorporations, Religious Societies, Volumes A - C. (Vol. C was current in 1964); Merzbacher, John S., Trenton's Foreign Colonies. Tren¬ton: Press of Beers & Frey, 1908; Paul Teicher, "The Dr. Herzl Zion Hebrew School, a History, 1883-1964," appearing in the School's Scholar¬ship Dinner Journal, January 31, 1964, Trenton, N. J.; and interviews with Mr. Leon Kasman, in 1966; Harry J. Podmore, Trenton – Old and New, Trenton Historical society, (Trenton: Kenneth W. Moore Company, 1927).. Accessed June15, 2012

Hadassa Word Press

More Books!

yes **I want** morebooks!

Buy your books fast and straightforward online - at one of the world's fastest growing online book stores! Environmentally sound due to Print-on-Demand technologies.

Buy your books online at
www.get-morebooks.com

Kaufen Sie Ihre Bücher schnell und unkompliziert online – auf einer der am schnellsten wachsenden Buchhandelsplattformen weltweit!
Dank Print-On-Demand umwelt- und ressourcenschonend produziert.

Bücher schneller online kaufen
www.morebooks.de

OmniScriptum Marketing DEU GmbH
Bahnhofstraße 28
66111 Saarbrücken, Deutschland
Telefax: +49 681 37 20 174-9

info@omniscriptum.com
www.omniscriptum.com

OMNIScriptum

30909427R00088

Made in the USA
Middletown, DE
11 April 2016